I MOVED TO LOS ANGELES TO WORK IN ANIMATION™

NATALIE NOURIGAT

BOOM! BOX™

Designer
KARA LEOPARD

Associate Editor
SOPHIE PHILIPS-ROBERTS

Editor
SHANNON WATTERS

BOOM! BOX™

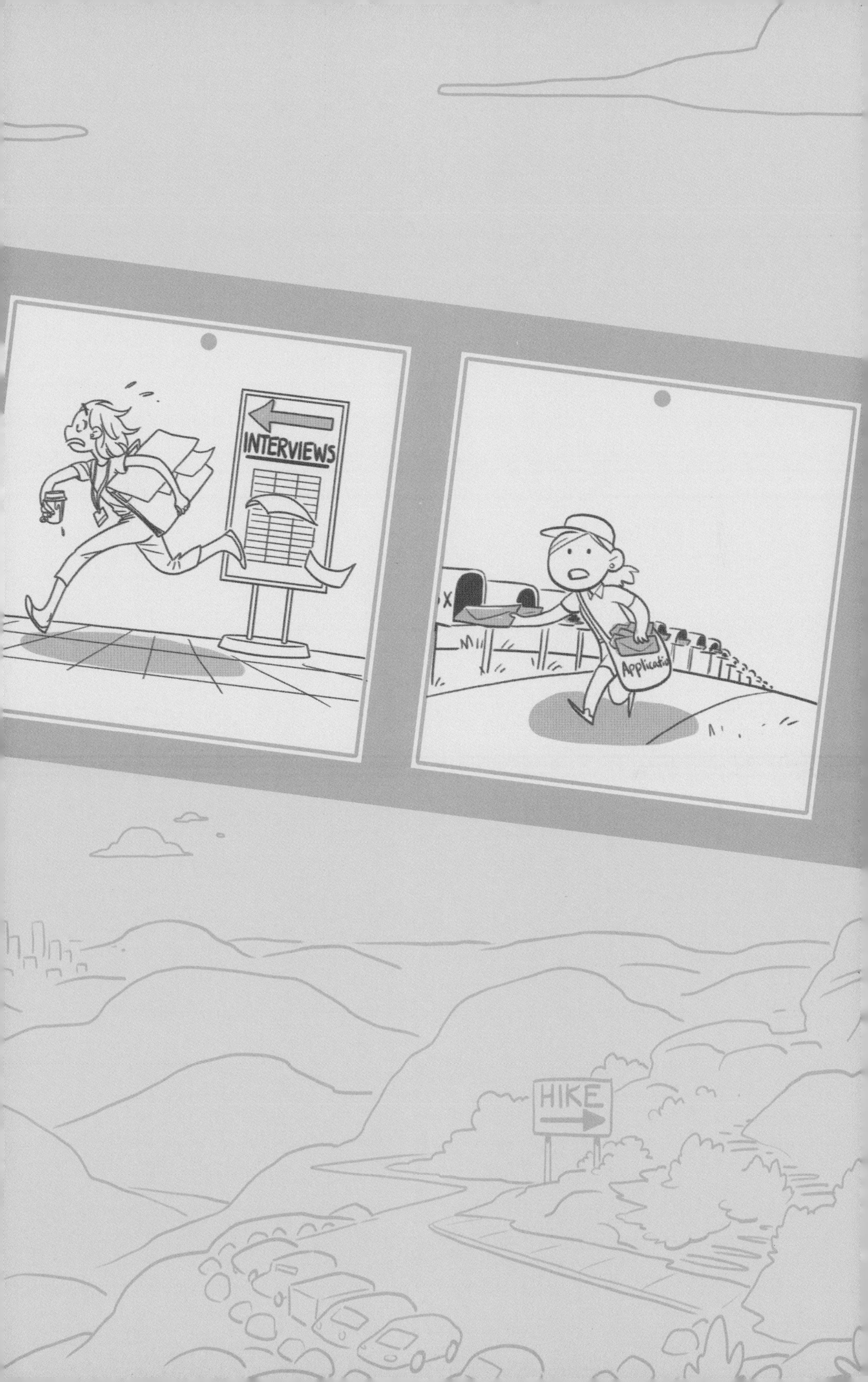
INTERVIEWS
Application
HIKE

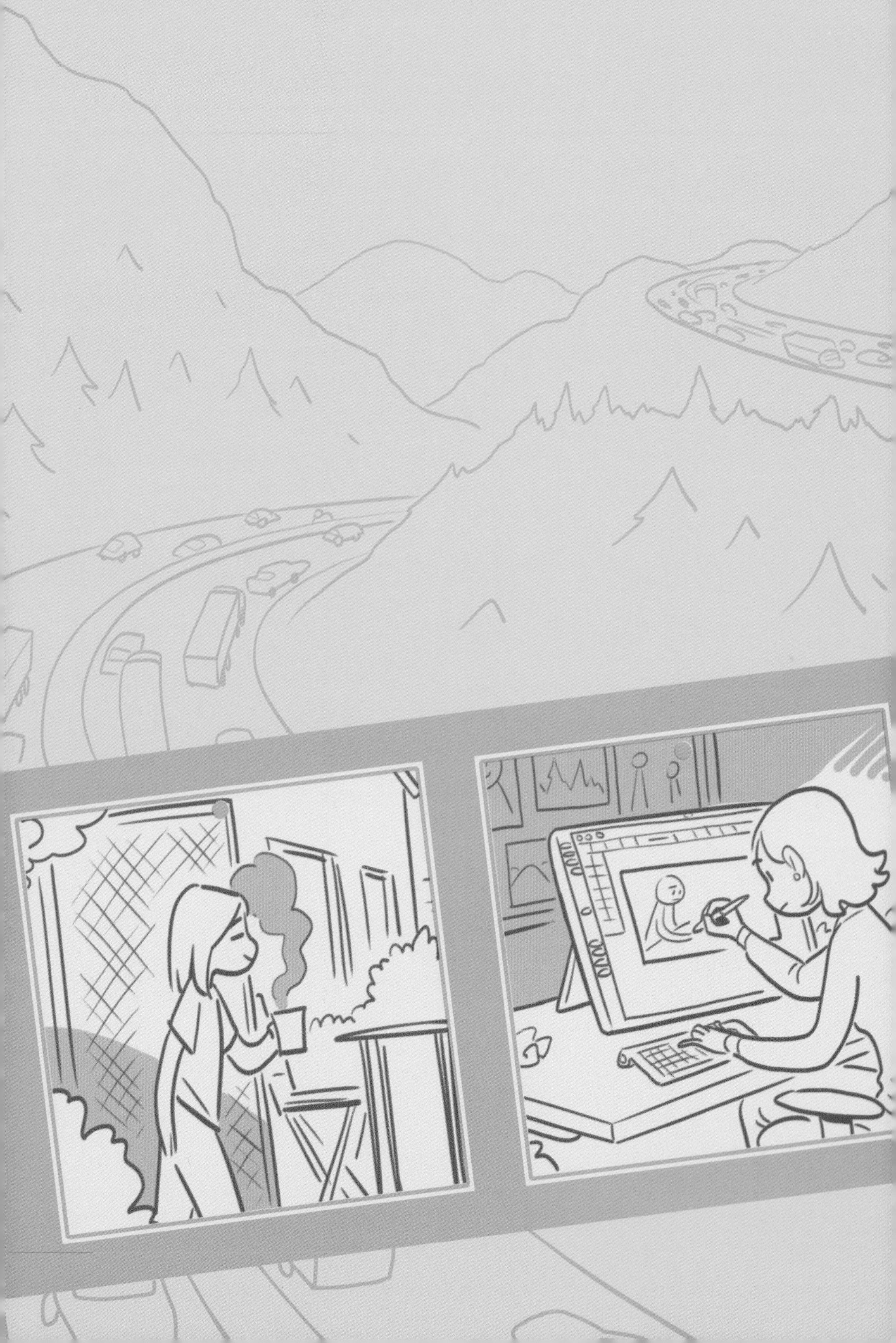

Written & Illustrated by
NATALIE NOURIGAT

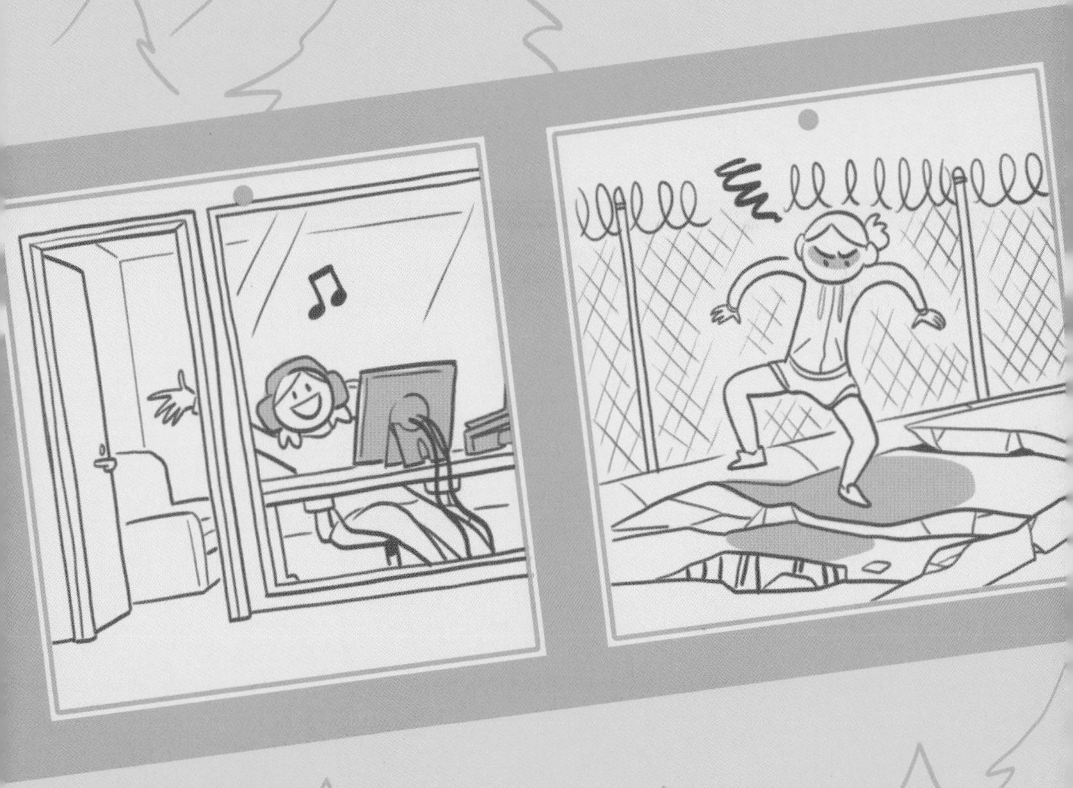

Disclaimer

THIS IS JUST ONE PERSON'S EXPERIENCE FROM WORKING IN A FEW STUDIOS, PLUS WHAT I HAVE HEARD FROM FRIENDS AT VARIOUS STUDIOS. IT IS ALL COLORED BY MY BACKGROUND, IDENTITY, AND PRIVILEGE. I AM GOING TO SAY SOME THINGS THAT ARE JUST MY OPINION. SOME PEOPLE WILL DISAGREE WITH ME (WELCOME TO EARTH).

I STILL WANT TO SHARE MY STORY, IN THE HOPES THAT THERE WILL BE INFORMATION IN HERE THAT HELPS PEOPLE CONSIDERING A SIMILAR MOVE / CAREER PATH. IT CAN BE REALLY HARD TO FIND SPECIFIC INFORMATION ABOUT WORKING IN ANIMATION, SO I WANT TO ADD MY LITTLE DATA SAMPLE TO THE PUBLIC COLLECTION.

SEEK OUT ADVICE FROM LOTS OF DIFFERENT PEOPLE TO GET THE FULL PICTURE!

Introduction

IF YOU WORK IN ANIMATION, YOU HAVE PROBABLY CONSIDERED A MOVE TO LOS ANGELES. THAT'S WHERE MOST OF THE AMERICAN ANIMATION INDUSTRY IS : CARTOON NETWORK, DISNEY, DREAMWORKS, FOX, HASBRO, JIBJAB, MARVEL, NICKELODEON, PARAMOUNT, SONY, SOUTH PARK STUDIOS, TITMOUSE, WARNER BROS., AND MORE.

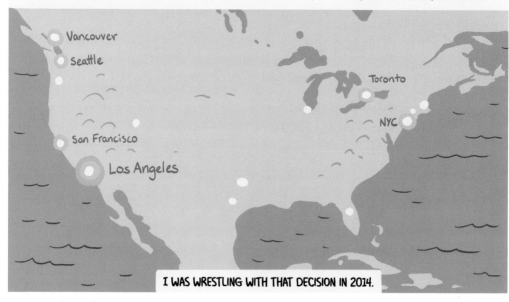

Vancouver

Seattle

Toronto

NYC

San Francisco

Los Angeles

I WAS WRESTLING WITH THAT DECISION IN 2014.

I'M FROM PORTLAND, OREGON. I COULDN'T JUSTIFY THE COST OF ART SCHOOL, SO I WENT TO A STATE UNIVERSITY AND STUDIED JAPANESE AND BUSINESS. YOU KNOW, TO GET A "REAL" JOB.

AFTER COLLEGE I WAS ABLE TO MAKE A LIVING DRAWING COMICS, SO I DID THAT INSTEAD. PORTLAND WAS MORE AFFORDABLE IN 2010. I WORKED IN AN AWESOME STUDIO OF FREELANCERS DOWNTOWN. THEY TAUGHT ME HOW TO MAKE LOTS MORE MONEY BY DRAWING COMMERCIAL STORYBOARDS PART-TIME.

AFTER 3 YEARS OF BURNING THE MIDNIGHT OIL, RICE, BEANS, AND $2 PBRS, I EVEN SAVED ENOUGH MONEY TO LIVE ABROAD FOR A YEAR!

I want to teach English in Japan and draw comics at night! ♥

I'll be working as an AU PAIR and couch-surfing, but STILL!!! It's always been a dream of mine to live abroad...! ♥♥

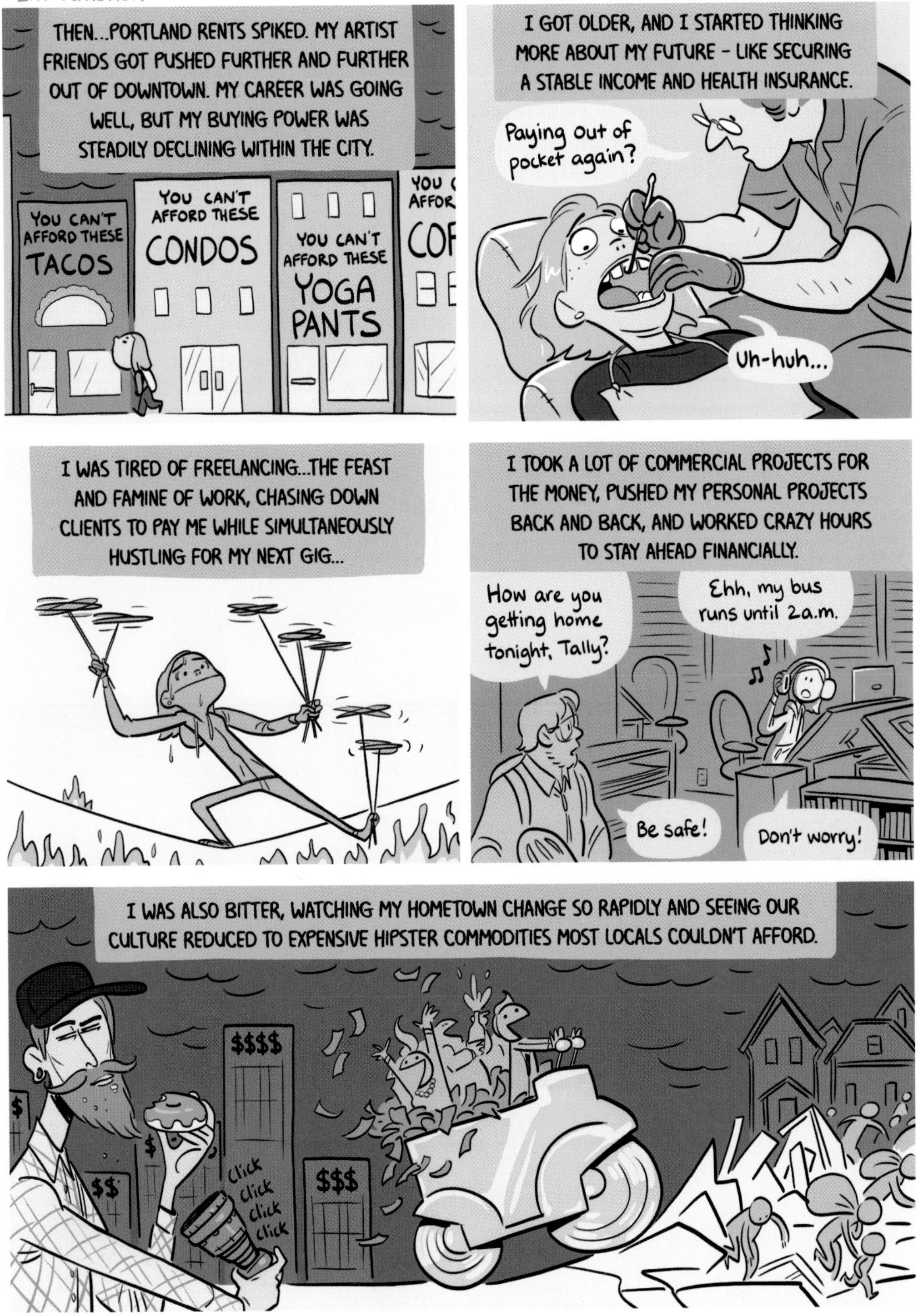
THEN...PORTLAND RENTS SPIKED. MY ARTIST FRIENDS GOT PUSHED FURTHER AND FURTHER OUT OF DOWNTOWN. MY CAREER WAS GOING WELL, BUT MY BUYING POWER WAS STEADILY DECLINING WITHIN THE CITY.
YOU CAN'T AFFORD THESE TACOS
YOU CAN'T AFFORD THESE CONDOS
YOU CAN'T AFFORD THESE YOGA PANTS
I GOT OLDER, AND I STARTED THINKING MORE ABOUT MY FUTURE – LIKE SECURING A STABLE INCOME AND HEALTH INSURANCE.
Paying out of pocket again?
Uh-huh...
I WAS TIRED OF FREELANCING...THE FEAST AND FAMINE OF WORK, CHASING DOWN CLIENTS TO PAY ME WHILE SIMULTANEOUSLY HUSTLING FOR MY NEXT GIG...
I TOOK A LOT OF COMMERCIAL PROJECTS FOR THE MONEY, PUSHED MY PERSONAL PROJECTS BACK AND BACK, AND WORKED CRAZY HOURS TO STAY AHEAD FINANCIALLY.
How are you getting home tonight, Tally?
Ehh, my bus runs until 2a.m.
Be safe!
Don't worry!
I WAS ALSO BITTER, WATCHING MY HOMETOWN CHANGE SO RAPIDLY AND SEEING OUR CULTURE REDUCED TO EXPENSIVE HIPSTER COMMODITIES MOST LOCALS COULDN'T AFFORD.
$$$$
$
$$
$
$$$
click click click click

DURING THIS TIME, A BUNCH OF CARTOONISTS I KNEW MOVED FROM PORTLAND TO L.A. FOR LUCRATIVE ANIMATION JOBS THAT USED SIMILAR SKILLS AS COMICS : STORYBOARDING, CHARACTER DESIGN, PROP DESIGN, EFX DESIGN, LAYOUT ART, BACKGROUND PAINTING, COLOR STYLING, VISUAL DEVELOPMENT ART, ETC.

♪ seems it never rains in Southern California ♪

THEIR UPDATES FROM L.A. SEEMED PRETTY GREAT...

sniff

AND AN ANIMATION INDUSTRY JOB SEEMED LIKE ONE OF THE FEW WAYS AN ARTIST COULD DRAW STORIES FOR A LIVING AND HAVE SOME FINANCIAL STABILITY...

I WANTED TO TRY WORKING IN ANIMATION, BUT I HESITATED TO MAKE THE MOVE TO L.A. FOR A LONG TIME. I HAD **FEARS** ABOUT L.A....

NO TREES?

POLLUTION?

COCKROACHES?

CRIME?

GANGS?

SMOG?

UGLY CITY?

EARTHQUAKES?

TOO SKETCHY TO WALK ALONE?

DROUGHT?

FAKE PEOPLE?

EXPENSIVE?

CAN I HACK IT IN A NEW INDUSTRY?

SEEDY STUFF?

GROSS WATER?

FAR FROM FAMILY & FRIENDS?

CAN I MAKE NEW FRIENDS?

CULTS?

DIFFERENT CULTURE?

sniff

MY FRIEND MADDY OFFERED TO HOST ME FOR A FEW DAYS SO I COULD SEE WHAT LIFE WAS REALLY LIKE IN L.A. FOR A CARTOONIST.

SHE SHOWED ME HER LIFE, TALKED TO ME ABOUT HER TRANSITION FROM PORTLAND, AND INTRODUCED ME TO PEOPLE AT A COUPLE OF STUDIOS. EVERYONE I MET WAS REALLY DOWN TO EARTH AND NICE.

THE WEATHER WAS ABSOLUTELY BEAUTIFUL, WARM ENOUGH TO WEAR JUST A T-SHIRT IN NOVEMBER!

WE WATCHED WRESTLING WITH A DOZEN CARTOONISTS WHO LIVED NEARBY.

WE WENT TO LITTLE TOKYO.

WE WENT TO THE BEACH. (IN NOVEMBER!!!)

MADDY WORKED ON HER OWN COMICS PROJECTS IN THE EVENINGS AFTER WORK.

HER LIFE WAS GREAT. IT REASSURED ME TO SEE THAT WITH MY OWN EYES.

I'LL NEVER FORGET THE MOMENT I DECIDED I COULD LIVE IN L.A.

DRINKING MY COFFEE IN HER FRONT GARDEN ON A NOVEMBER MORNING WARM ENOUGH FOR A T-SHIRT...

PETTING THE FRIENDLY STRAY CAT AND SMELLING THE BLOOMING FLOWERS...

Yeah... I could live like this.

SO THEN IT WAS JUST A MATTER OF GETTING A JOB IN AN L.A. ANIMATION STUDIO! ...RIGHT?

HA HA HA HA HA HA HA HA HA HA HA

Right, "just get a job in a studio"!

Getting a Job

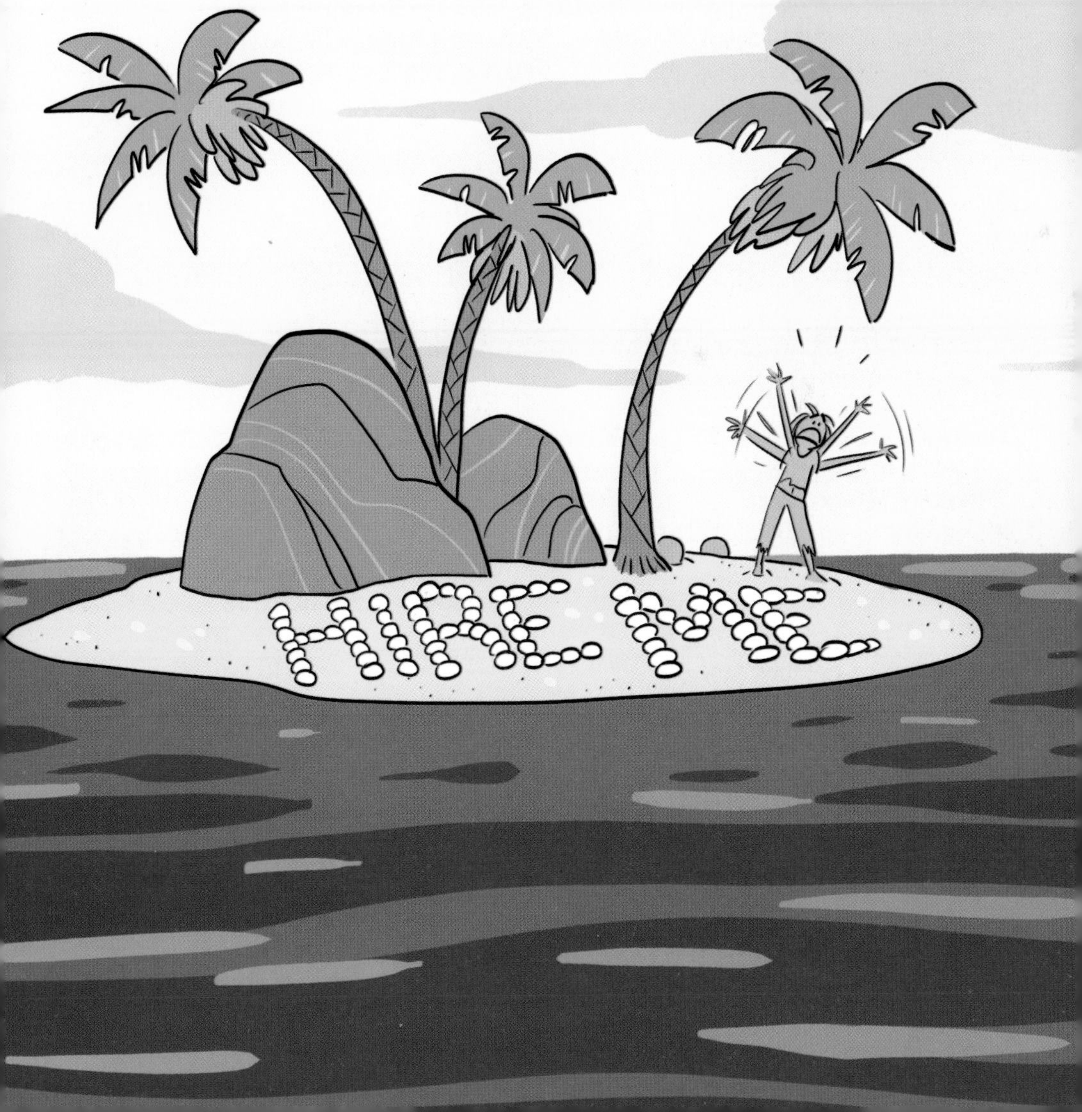
HIRE ME

AT THAT POINT, I HAD ALREADY BEEN APPLYING TO STORY POSITIONS AND INTERNSHIPS FOR **7 YEARS**...AND I HAD NOTHING TO SHOW FOR IT.

Is this because I don't go to an art school?

2009

All of these jobs require experience...

2011

Am I too OLD now??

2013

I HAD NEARLY GIVEN UP ON THIS EVER HAPPENING FOR ME, BUT I WAS SO FIRED UP ABOUT ANIMATION (AND WORRIED ABOUT MY FUTURE IF I STAYED IN PORTLAND), I DECIDED TO GIVE IT ONE LAST BIG EFFORT AND SEE IF I COULD MAKE SOMETHING HAPPEN.

I STARTED SERIOUSLY APPLYING TO JOBS IN OCTOBER 2014. "SERIOUSLY" MEANING : JOB-HUNTING TOOK UP ABOUT HALF OF MY DAY. I CHECKED EACH STUDIO'S WEBSITE **AND** AGGREGATE JOB SITES FIRST THING EVERY MORNING. I APPLIED TO ANYTHING RELEVANT AS QUICKLY AS I COULD, THAT DAY IF POSSIBLE.

I COMPARED WHAT THEY WERE LOOKING FOR TO MY CV AND PORTFOLIO. IF THEY WANTED TO SEE ZOO SKETCHES AND I DIDN'T HAVE ANY RECENT ONES IN MY PORTFOLIO, I'D GO TO THE ZOO THAT WEEKEND AND DRAW SOME NEW SAMPLES TO PUT IN MY PORTFOLIO.

I TOOK A STORYBOARDING CLASS AT THE LOCAL FILM SCHOOL, HIT THE LIBRARY FOR FILM STUDIES BOOKS, JOINED LYNDA.COM, TOOK A BUNCH OF ONLINE CLASSES FOR ANIMATION SOFTWARE AND STORY-BOARDING, AND SCOURED THE INTERNET FOR FREE TUTORIALS. I MADE **TONS** OF NEW ART.

Getting a Job

I ALREADY HAD 5 YEARS UNDER MY BELT AS A PROFESSIONAL COMIC BOOK ARTIST AND FREELANCE STORYBOARD ARTIST, BUT IT TOOK MORE THAN A YEAR OF AGGRESSIVE JOB-SEARCHING BEFORE I STARTED WORKING IN A STUDIO.

An email from (studio)!!! "Dear Applicant..."

YOU COULD BE LUCKIER OR UN-LUCKIER THAN ME, BUT MY ADVICE TO ANYONE LOOKING FOR THEIR FIRST STUDIO JOB IS : BUCKLE UP AND PREPARE FOR A LONG JOB-HUNTING PROCESS, AND TREAT IT SERIOUSLY.

"...we regret to inform you..."

Dang it.

I APPLIED TO 28 POSITIONS OVER THAT YEAR. 3 OF THEM GAVE ME STORY TESTS, WHICH EACH TOOK WEEKS TO COMPLETE. I HAD TO MAINTAIN MY NORMAL WORK-LOAD ON TOP OF THAT, AND MAKE ENOUGH MONEY TO STAY AFLOAT.

Ughh...

"WHAT'S A STORY TEST?"

A "STORY TEST" COULD BE ANYTHING FROM A SAMPLE SCRIPT YOU HAVE TO STORYBOARD, TO BRAINSTORMING GAGS, TO A PROMPT OFF OF WHICH YOU HAVE TO WRITE AND BOARD YOUR OWN ORIGINAL SHORT STORY. FOR EXAMPLE...

"BOARD A SCENE WHERE SOMEONE GOES ON A DATE, AND EVERYTHING THAT CAN POSSIBLY GO WRONG GOES WRONG."

"CHARACTERS **A** AND **B** ARE SINGING A SONG ABOUT HOMEWORK. WRITE SOME FUNNY LYRICS FOR THEM."

"MAKE UP TWO CHARACTERS WHO ARE OPPOSITES. STORY-BOARD A SEQUENCE WHERE THEY MEET FOR THE FIRST TIME."

ADVICE FROM FRIENDS IN THE INDUSTRY :

If you're getting story tests, that means your drawing skills are good enough. Now it's just about finding the right fit — a show that has the same sense of humor as you, a studio that's hiring at the right time, or making a friend in the right place. Hang in there!

H...how long does this part normally take?

NOD

I've known some people that got the job from their first story test, and I had a friend who didn't get a job offer until her 30th story test.

HOOOLY... I hope it doesn't take me 30 story tests...

Getting a Job

I WENT INTO MY JOB SEARCH OVERLY CONFIDENT, HOPING FOR A STORYBOARD ARTIST POSITION RIGHT OFF THE BAT. I ALREADY DREW COMICS AND COMMERCIAL STORYBOARDS -- HOW DIFFERENT COULD STORYBOARDING FOR ANIMATION BE?

Pretty different, it turns out.

STORYBOARDS FOR ANIMATION TURNED OUT TO BE VERY LOOSE DRAWINGS, LESS ABOUT TECHNIQUE AND MORE ABOUT GETTING STORY IDEAS ACROSS CLEARLY WITH STRONG EMOTIONAL IMPACT.

HUNDREDS OF DRAWINGS, **LOOSE** AND GESTURAL, WITH SOME GRAY TO ADD DEPTH IF TIME ALLOWS. LOTS OF CONSTRUCTION LINES AND MISTAKES LEFT IN.

MOST COMMERCIAL "STORYBOARDS" ARE MORE LIKE **ILLUSTRATIONS** MEANT TO SELL COMMERCIALS.

4-6 DRAWINGS, VERY CLEAN, IN COLOR, OFTEN STIFF & REALISTIC

THE CAMERA ALSO CONFOUNDED ME. IN COMICS, I JUST PUT IT WHEREVER I COULD GET A COMPOSITION I LIKED. IN FILM, IT WAS A CHARACTER UNTO ITSELF, AND MOVED ACCORDING TO LOTS OF RULES.

AS TIME WORE ON AND I HAD NO LUCK, I RE-FOCUSED MY JOB SEARCH ON MORE ENTRY-LEVEL POSITIONS. A LOT OF STUDIOS OFFERED ENTRY-LEVEL POSITIONS LIKE "STORYBOARD REVISIONIST" OR INTERN / TRAINING PROGRAMS.

I GOT TURNED DOWN FOR A STORY ARTIST POSITION AT A FEATURE ANIMATION STUDIO...

Noooooooo

...BUT THE RECRUITER SUGGESTED I APPLY FOR AN UPCOMING TRAINING POSITION IN THE STORY DEPARTMENT.

Hm?

Is it PAID?

Yes

Alright!

Getting a Job

AND SO...

5 ½ MONTHS AFTER INITIALLY BEING CONTACTED...

3 ½ MONTHS AFTER TURNING IN MY RESUME AND PORTFOLIO...

1 MONTH AFTER COMPLETING THEIR STORY TEST...

2 DAYS AFTER A VIDEO CALL INTERVIEW...

BRING BRING!

Incoming Call

Hi! This is (recruiter) from (studio)! Is this a good time to talk?

Y-Yes!

OH MY GOD I GOT THE JOB

How soon can you start?

Moving

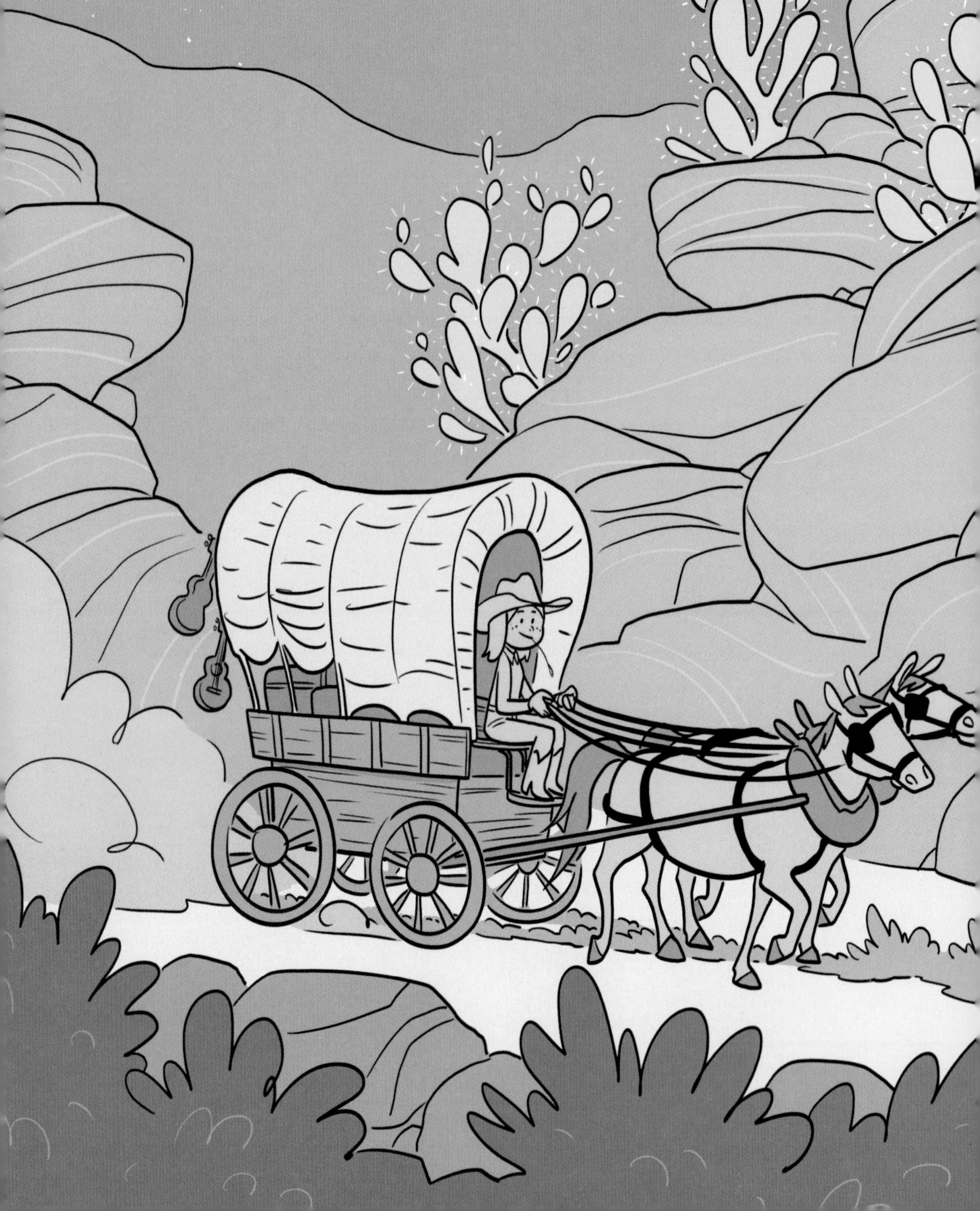

Moving

THE STUDIO WANTED ME TO START 2 WEEKS LATER. I ASKED FOR 4 WEEKS AND THEY AGREED.
IT WAS STILL A PRETTY SHORT TIMEFRAME TO ORGANIZE A MOVE TO ANOTHER STATE.

I WASN'T ABLE TO FIND HOUSING FROM AFAR, SO I ASKED MY FRIEND JAMIE IF I COULD COUCH-SURF WITH HIM FOR A FEW WEEKS WHEN I ARRIVED.

Sigh, fine.

THEN THINGS STARTED HAPPENING VERY QUICKLY. I LET MY FREELANCE CLIENTS KNOW THAT I WAS LEAVING, AND FINISHED UP MY GIGS WITH THEM. I BOUGHT MY FIRST CAR...

$12,000 in debt...
$12,000 in debt...

I really hope this job works out...

I GOT RID OF MOST OF MY POSSESSIONS, AND PACKED UP WHAT I WAS KEEPING

Take care of my babies, Terry!

NOD

COM
COMICS

I SAID GOODBYE TO MY PORTLAND FRIENDS AND FAMILY.

...AND DROVE EVERYTHING I OWNED DOWN TO L.A.

Il me semble que la misère

Serait moins penible au soleil~!

(A.K.A. "2 DAYS ALONE ON I-5, SINGING AND CRYING")

AFTER WORK, I HOUSE-HUNTED. I COULD ONLY VISIT PROPERTIES AFTER 7PM, AND IT WAS VERY COMPETITIVE. PLUS, I DIDN'T KNOW THE NEIGHBORHOODS. IT WAS...DISCOURAGING.

A 45 Walk Score... It's right next to a highway...carpets smell like pee...no view...I can already hear the neighbors... how can they be asking $1300/mo for this place...?

Miss?

Thank you for coming to look, but we already have SEVERAL applications in, so...

!

What the hell? That listing JUST went up yesterday!

FOR RENT

AFTER WEEKS OF FRUITLESS SEARCHING, HERE'S HOW I GOT MY FIRST L.A. APARTMENT :

Jamie, do you like the company that manages your apartment?

Yeah.

I'm just gonna call them...

Hello, I'm looking for a 1-bedroom apartment for less than $1500/mo in Burbank or NoHo, do you have anything like that available?

Not right now, but if you submit an application, we can call you when something is about to hit the market, and you can get a head-start to apply for it.

Sounds good!

A WEEK LATER, I SIGNED THE LEASE ON A MEDIOCRE APARTMENT.

It has cheap floors, unsealed windows, a rusty little stove, ants, a gas smell...

...BUT, I'm right next to the ocean!

What?? No way!

Yeah, I'm looking at it right now! I'll send you a pic...

THE OCEAN AUTO REPAIR

CLANG CLANG WHIRRRRR

^I told this joke waaaaaaay too many times.

IF I HAD IT TO DO OVER, I WOULD COUCH-SURF OR SUBLET AROUND THE CITY FOR A COUPLE OF MONTHS AND GIVE MYSELF MORE TIME TO LOOK FOR THE RIGHT APARTMENT / NEIGHBORHOOD BEFORE COMMITTING.

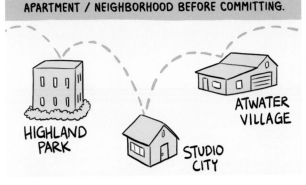

HIGHLAND PARK

STUDIO CITY

ATWATER VILLAGE

For house-hunting tools, I use Padmapper, Hotpads, Craigslist, and Zillow Rentals.

I ASKED ONE OF MY FRIENDS HOW SHE SCORED HER SWEET APARTMENT IN LOS FELIZ AND SHE SAID:

I went to Craigslist listings without photos that no one else showed up to. It's a crap-shoot, but sometimes the landlord just isn't tech-savy, and you can get lucky!

ONE SURPRISING THING ABOUT HOUSE-HUNTING IN L.A.: OFTEN, PROPERTIES FOR RENT ARE LEFT EMPTY AND UNLOCKED, SO YOU JUST LET YOURSELF IN TO CHECK THEM OUT.

Feels sketchy, but OK...

FOR RENT

A LOT OF THE ANIMATION STUDIOS ARE IN SAN FERNANDO VALLEY, SO A LOT OF ANIMATION FOLKS LIVE NEARBY, EVEN THOUGH THERE ARE CHEAPER AND NICER AREAS TO LIVE.

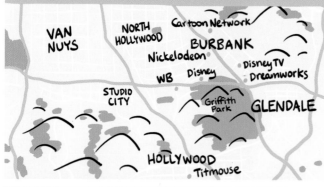

VAN NUYS

NORTH HOLLYWOOD

Cartoon Network

BURBANK

Nickelodeon

WB   Disney

Disney TV
Dreamworks

STUDIO CITY

Griffith Park

GLENDALE

HOLLYWOOD
Titmouse

I LIVE LESS THAN 5 MILES FROM WORK, AND IT'S 100% WORTH IT TO ME. I DON'T WANT TO SPEND HOURS DRIVING EVERY DAY.

I can practically see the studio from my driveway.

There's affordable stuff scattered throughout most areas, but I would say NoHo, Burbank, Glendale, Studio City, and Van Nuys are some affordable areas very close to the studios to check out.

I couch-surfed in NoHo first, then I lived near the Universal City Metro stop, and now I'm in Burbank. They're all fine, but I prefer Burbank for the quieter setting with more green/trees.

There are also affordable listings downtown in Hollywood and Koreatown, but I don't have experience living in those areas.

HEADS UP : APARTMENTS OFTEN COME WITHOUT REFRIGERATORS IN L.A.! I HAD TO BUY MINE, AND WHEN I MOVED OUT, THE APARTMENT REFUSED TO KEEP MY LIKE-NEW FRIDGE!

Great. Now I have to hire movers...

ANOTHER HEADS UP : EVEN THOUGH I'M VERY ENERGY-CONSCIOUS, I NEED A/C HERE. THERE ARE A FEW WEEKS IN THE SUMMER THAT WOULD BE REALLY AWFUL WITHOUT A/C.

Perks of Working in Animation Guild Studios**

WORK CONDITIONS AT ANIMATION GUILD SHOPS ARE NEGOTIATED BY THE ANIMATION GUILD (OR "T.A.G."), A UNION FOR ARTISTS IN ANIMATION.

A single artist doesn't have much negotiating power against a huge corporation with an army of lawyers, but by banding together we command respect and raise working conditions.

HISTORY CORNER : IN 1941, AFTER A 5-WEEK STRIKE, DISNEY RECOGNIZED THE SCREEN CARTOONIST GUILD (WHICH WOULD LATER BECOME T.A.G.), RAISING WAGES, ESTABLISHING A 40-HOUR WORK WEEK, AND GIVING SCREEN CREDITS TO ARTISTS. IT ALSO PAVED THE WAY FOR A LATER PENSION PLAN AND HEALTHCARE PLAN.

NOW, THERE ARE STRICT RULES ABOUT MINIMUM WAGES, OVERTIME, THE NUMBER OF DAYS IN A ROW A STUDIO CAN MAKE US WORK, VACATION TIME, SICK TIME, SEVERANCE PAY, SCREEN CREDIT, UNEMPLOYMENT, ETC. THERE IS AN AUTOMATIC, EMPLOYER-FUNDED PENSION PLAN, AN OPTIONAL 401(K) PLAN, AND A GREAT EMPLOYER-FUNDED HEALTHCARE PLAN. THE GUILD CAN ALSO ACT AS AN ADVOCATE IF A MEMBER HAS A DISPUTE WITH THEIR EMPLOYER.

I feel supported, like I have people in my corner.

T.A.G. MEMBERS HAVE THE OPTION TO ATTEND MONTHLY MEETINGS TO DISCUSS RELEVANT WORKPLACE ISSUES.

It's very empowering to discuss "taboo" things like money and work conditions with other artists, to make sure we aren't being taken advantage of.

How are we going to stop studios from giving us insane deadlines without approving us to work overtime hours??

Over the last few years, "Storyboarding" a scene has become writing, boarding, drawing key frames, and timing a scene. But we're still only paid for one job.

Perks of Working in TAG Studios

THERE ARE PLENTY OF ISSUES IN THIS INDUSTRY. WE HAVE TO STAY INFORMED AND ADVOCATE FOR OUR RIGHTS. THERE ARE SOME SERIOUSLY ABUSIVE PRACTICES OUT THERE. IT'S A GOOD IDEA TO TALK TO OTHER ARTISTS ABOUT THEIR EXPERIENCES.

Problem!

Past experience!

T.A.G. ALSO OFFERS REDUCED-RATE CLASSES TO TEACH SPECIFIC ANIMATION JOB SKILLS LIKE STORYBOARDING, DRAWING IN PERSPECTIVE, DIGITAL PAINTING, ETC.

I get T.A.G.'s monthly bulletin with the latest news, events, and class offerings.

I called T.A.G. a lot in the beginning, whenever I had questions about paperwork, or my rights, or membership fees. I always got a helpful person on the phone right away.

Hello, Animation Guild.

I'M VERY HAPPY TO BE IN A UNION JOB AFTER YEARS IN THE WILD WEST OF FREELANCING, WITH RANDOM HOURS AND THE FEELING THAT IF I SAY "NO" TO AN EMPLOYER THEY CAN REPLACE ME IMMEDIATELY.

Heyyy, we're actually gonna need more fixes on those boards we approved earlier today...

11PM ON A SATURDAY:

Okie-doke!

...And the pitch is first thing tomorrow, so send them ASAP tonight, OK?

You got it!

IT'S ALSO A BIG DEAL TO ME THAT MY STARTING INCOME HERE MORE THAN DOUBLED WHAT I WAS MAKING WITH A GOOD FREELANCE CAREER IN PORTLAND.

Woah... I might actually be able to afford a house someday...

AND I HAVE HEALTH INSURANCE, INCLUDING DENTAL, VISION, AND BEHAVIORAL HEALTH!

YAY!

You also have 8 cavities.

Aww.

SOME STUDIOS OFFER BENEFITS BEYOND THE MINIMUM. I CAN'T BELIEVE SOME OF THE PERKS I'VE HAD :

FREE FOOD!

I save so much money by eating free cereal, fruit, and coffee at the studio!

SCREENINGS, Q+A'S WITH DIRECTORS, WRITERS, ETC.

CONTINUING ART EDUCATION!
LIFE DRAWING, ACCESS TO SOFTWARE, SUBSCRIPTIONS TO TUTORIAL SITES, FREE CLASSES AND LECTURES, AND EDUCATIONAL ENHANCEMENT ACTIVITIES OF OUR CHOICE.

ON-SITE GAS & CARWASHES

Coco Corolla, you look fantastic!

DAYCARE

Mommy has to go back to her Cintiq now! I'll visit again later!

IN-BUILDING MASSAGE THERAPISTS AND ERGONOMIC EVALUATIONS

Help

GYMS & FREE ATHLETIC CLASSES

COMMUNITY!
GROUP LUNCHES, GIFT EXCHANGES, AND DEPARTMENT PARTIES. STUDIOS CAN HOST THINGS LIKE SUMMER BBQS AND OSCAR-WATCHING PARTIES.

MENTORSHIP, REGULAR FEEDBACK, AND INSPIRATION FROM THE REEEALLY TALENTED PEOPLE ALSO WORKING THERE.

NOD

SWAAAAAAAAG

A Day in the Life

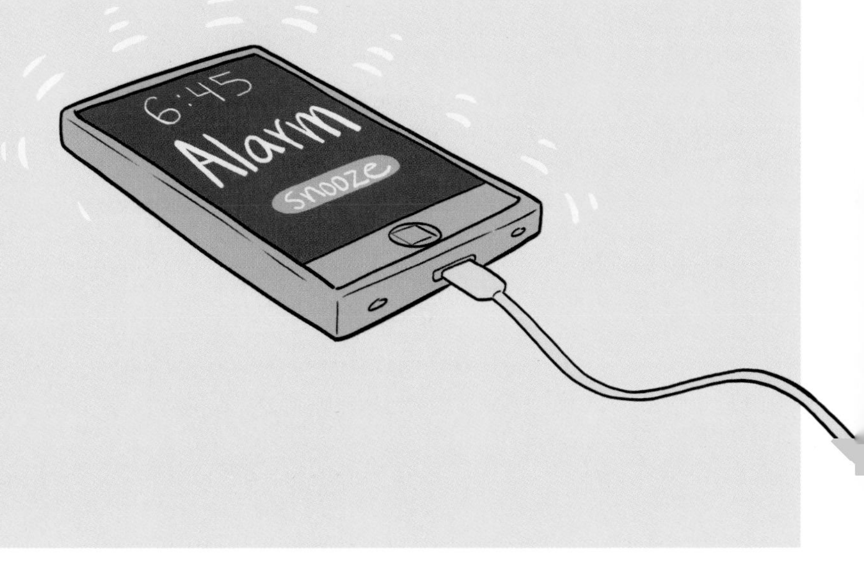
6:45
Alarm
Snooze

A Day in the Life

"WHAT'S A TYPICAL DAY LIKE?"

I work about 45 hours per week, 9:00a.m.– 7:00p.m. Monday– Friday, with an hour for lunch.

There's a cafeteria with lots of breakfast and lunch options — about $6 for a made-to-order breakfast omelet, $3 for soup, $9 for a fish and veggie lunch. I take it back to my desk if I'm in a crunch, but I eat with the other artists whenever possible.

I SNACK ON FREE CEREAL, FRUIT, TEA, AND COFFEE.

It takes calories to make art, you know.

IF I HAVE TO WORK UNTIL 8 PM OR LATER, MY STUDIO BUYS ME DELIVERY DINNER.

I OFTEN GO TO LECTURES, LIFE DRAWING, OR SCREENINGS FOR 1–2 HOURS DURING THE LUNCH "HOUR".

I don't feel like I'm under a microscope at work. As long as I meet my deadlines, attend the meetings I am supposed to, and keep an eye on my email, it doesn't seem to be a problem to come in a little late or take long lunches.

THERE ARE OTHER MEETINGS LIKE DEPARTMENT MEETINGS, CHECK-INS WITH MY SUPERVISOR, STUDIO UPDATES, ETC.

Business Stuff

EVEN THOUGH THEY AREN'T MANDATORY, I GO TO OTHER STORY ARTISTS' PITCHES WHENEVER POSSIBLE. IT TEACHES ME A LOT TO SEE HOW OTHER PEOPLE DO IT.

STORY ARTISTS OFTEN PITCH DIGITALLY THESE DAYS, SO "PITCHING" MEANS CLICKING THROUGH A SERIES OF IMAGES PROJECTED FOR THE WHOLE ROOM, NARRATING ANY ACTION THAT NEEDS EXPLANATION, AND DOING THE VOICES FOR THE CHARACTERS. IT'S A BIT OF A PERFORMANCE, AND PEOPLE TEND TO LIKE IT WHEN ARTISTS ACT IT UP.

And then they go through the portal, WOOSH! And she's like, "WOAH!!"

IT'S AMAZING TO WATCH A PRO PITCH.

WHEN I GET LAUNCHED ON A NEW SCENE, I TALK THROUGH THE MATERIAL WITH MY TEAM. I GET TO ASK QUESTIONS AND PROPOSE IDEAS.

Shouldn't he be more surprised to see her on page 5?

THEN, I HAVE ABOUT A WEEK TO BOARD IT (ABOUT 100-500 DRAWINGS) AND PITCH IT TO THE SAME GROUP. I CAN GO TO MY TEAM FOR FEEDBACK ALONG THE WAY, OR FOR HELP IF I RUN INTO ISSUES.

I draw REALLY loose until I get approval to tie down my boards.

Like, stick figures with a background grid.

For most of the day I'm here, working in my office.

company Macbook & Cintiq →

STORY ARTISTS OFTEN GET ASKED TO QUICKLY CLEAN UP OR ALTER OUR OWN OR SOMEONE ELSE'S BOARDS. SOMETIMES THE SAME SCENE GETS REWORKED OVER AND OVER. WE HAVE TO BE FLEXIBLE AND NOT PRECIOUS WITH IT.

This week I'm going through the intro and coloring all the buildings blue.

Aha. I was the one who colored them red last month.

THERE'S ABOUT 10 STORY ARTISTS ON A MOVIE AT A TIME. I WORK ON A MOVIE AS LONG AS I'M NEEDED, WHICH COULD BE FOR THE WHOLE BOARDING PERIOD (ABOUT 18 MONTHS) OR A FEW WEEKS. THEN, WITH ANY LUCK, I "ROLL ONTO" ANOTHER MOVIE.

IF THERE'S A PERIOD WHERE I DON'T HAVE ANY ASSIGNMENTS, I PRACTICE DRAWING THE CHARACTERS FOR THE MOVIE I'M ON, OR TAKE PHOTOSHOP / BOARDING TUTORIALS, OR JUST REST AND GET READY FOR THE NEXT CRUNCH TIME.

Best Things About Living in L.A.

THE **WEATHER!**

You coming?

Yeah, just a minute!

FOOOD

WEARING OPEN-TOED SHOES AND LETTING MY UMBRELLA GATHER DUST. FORGETTING THAT I GET RAYNAUD'S SYMPTOMS.

WAKING UP TO THE SUN EVERY DAY. REDUCED SEASONAL AFFECTIVE DISORDER.

PRETTY SUNSETS EVERY NIGHT

THE BEACH

THE DESERT

NO MATTER THE MONTH, SOMETHING IS BLOOMING IN L.A. PALM TREES MAKE EVERY DAY FEEL LIKE A TROPICAL VACATION.

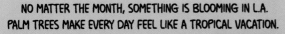

PLANTS FLOURISH HERE, ESPECIALLY SUCCULENTS. I COULDN'T KEEP SUCCULENTS ALIVE IN PORTLAND, BUT IN L.A. THEY GROW OUT OF CRACKS IN THE ALLEY!

THE LACK OF HUMIDITY. IF I CURL MY HAIR, IT STAYS CURLED ALL DAY. AND THE HEAT DOESN'T FEEL AS GROSS AS HUMID HEAT.

SUPER BONUS : THERE ARE ALMOST NO MOSQUITOES HERE!!!

L.A. IS A HUGE CITY, SO THERE'S A TON OF STUFF TO DO, TONS OF PEOPLE TO MEET, TONS OF COMIC SHOPS AND EVENTS AND COOL AREAS AND CONCERTS AND FOOD AND STAND-UP COMEDY AND IMPROV AND MUSEUMS AND ATTRACTIVE SINGLE PEOPLE! I'M NEVER BORED IF I KEEP AN OPEN MIND AND JUST GET OUT OF MY APARTMENT.

L.A.X. IS AN INTERNATIONAL HUB, SO IT'S BEEN EASIER TO SEE FRIENDS FROM FRANCE AND THE EAST COAST, AND MEET NEW PEOPLE FROM ALL OVER THE WORLD.

THE CHEESY HOLLYWOOD STUFF IS WEIRDLY FUN. I LOVE COMING OUT OF THE METRO AT HOLLYWOOD BLVD AND BEING SURPRISED BY A BIG TV OR FILM PREMIERE EVENT WITH THE RED CARPET OUT, ETC.

AND YOU KNOW....GROWING UP HEAVILY EXPOSED TO AMERICAN POP CULTURE, IT'S **FUN** TO SEE THE PLACES I'VE BEEN HEARING ABOUT AND SEEING IN MOVIES MY WHOLE LIFE!

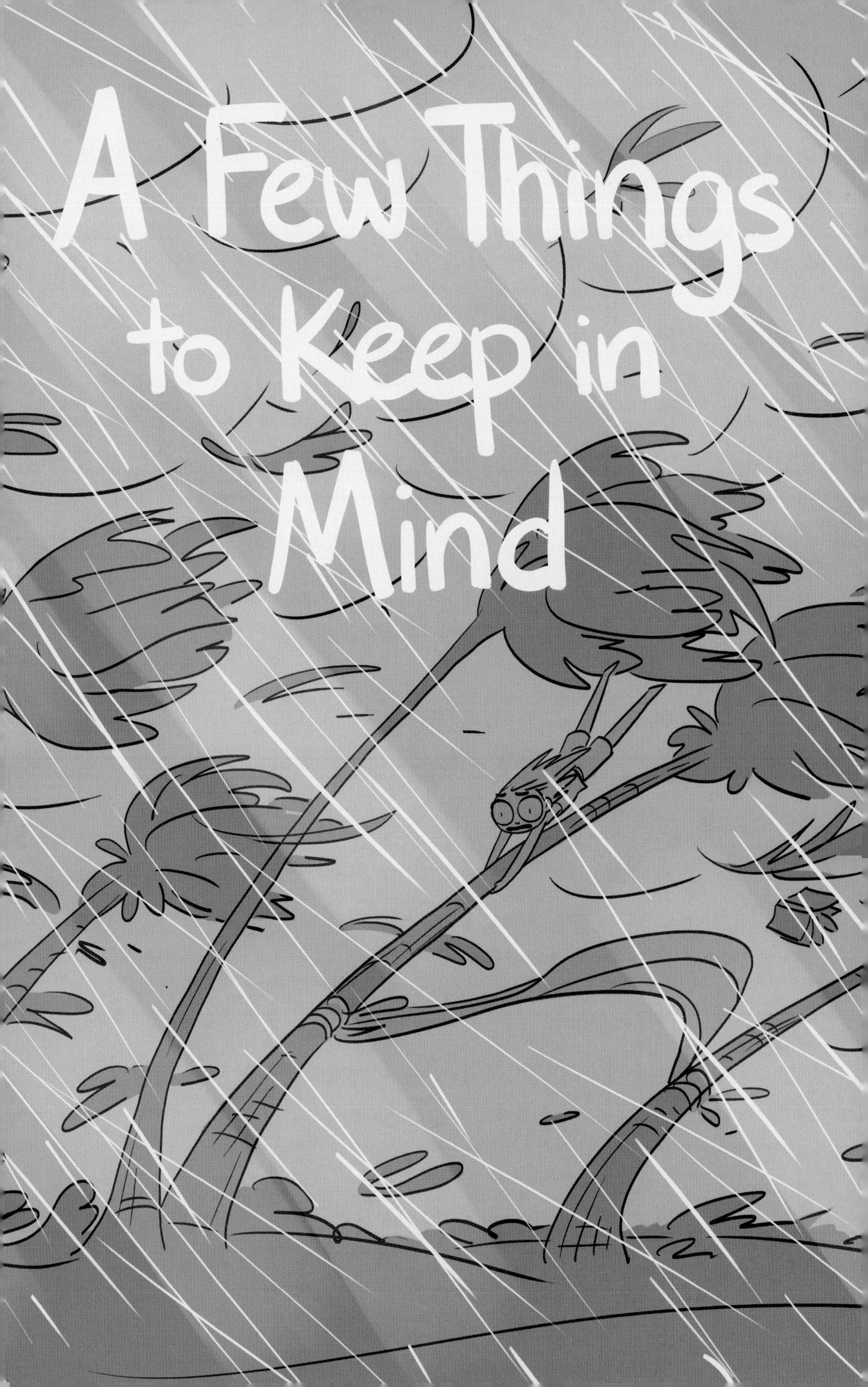
A Few Things to Keep in Mind

THE ANIMATION GUILD HAS A BIG, MANDATORY, UP-FRONT FEE TO BECOME A MEMBER — ABOUT 2 WEEKS' WAGES. SOME ANIMATION STUDIOS GIVE A SIGNING BONUS WHEN AN ARTIST BEGINS WORKING FOR THEM, WHICH THE ARTIST CAN USE HOWEVER THEY WANT, INCLUDING USING THAT SIGNING BONUS TO COVER THEIR T.A.G. FEES. THERE IS ALSO A $100 REGISTRATION FEE FOR IATSE, AND THERE ARE UNION DUES ($102.50 AT THE TIME OF THIS WRITING) DUE EVERY 3 MONTHS GOING FORWARD.

THE COST OF LIVING IN L.A. IS – YOU GUESSED IT – **HIGH**. SUBLET A ROOM : $800–$1200/MO. RENT A 1-BEDROOM APARTMENT NEAR THE STUDIOS : $1500/MO.

I KNOW SOME PEOPLE WHO HAVE MADE IT WORK HERE WITHOUT A CAR...

...BUT THE CITY SEEMS TO PUNISH ME WHEN I TRY TO GET AROUND WITHOUT A CAR. I DON'T THINK I'D BE HAPPY HERE WITHOUT ONE. I DON'T KNOW ANYONE WHO COMMUTES BY BUS OR TRAIN. PUBLIC TRANSPORTATION IN L.A. IS NOT ROBUST ENOUGH FOR MOST TRIPS.

I HAVE NO IDEA HOW SOMEONE IN A WHEELCHAIR WOULD NAVIGATE SOME OF THE CRAP THAT L.A. CALLS "SIDEWALKS" AND "STREETS".

I TRY TO ALWAYS PARK OFF OF THE STREET, AND I DON'T LEAVE MY CAR DOWNTOWN OVERNIGHT. TWO DIFFERENT FRIENDS OF MINE HERE HAVE WOKEN UP TO HIT-AND-RUN TOTALED CARS.

L.A. IS VERY INTO COSMETICS AND BEAUTY. I'VE NEVER LIVED SOMEWHERE WITH BILLBOARDS ADVERTISING LIPOSUCTION BEFORE. WHEN I GO TO SEE A DOCTOR, IT CAN BE REALLY FRUSTRATING DETERMINING WHAT IS HEALTHCARE AND WHAT IS JUST COSMETICS.

I went to the ENT and the brochures in the waiting room were advertising breast implants.

Should I find a new ENT??

SOMETIMES, L.A. FEELS LIKE THE CAPITOL IN THE HUNGER GAMES BOOKS. IT CAN BE INSULAR, GROSSLY MATERIALISTIC, UNAWARE OF HOW ABSURD IT IS TO THE OUTSIDE WORLD.

THERE IS SUCH WEALTH HERE, AND THERE IS SUCH POVERTY. PEOPLE BUY RIDICULOUSLY BIG HOUSES AND THEN BUILD TALL FENCES AND SPIKED GATES AROUND THEM AND POINT SECURITY CAMERAS AT THE STREET, IN CASE POOR PEOPLE WANT A PIECE OF THAT.

Maybe I sound like I'm complaining about the sky being blue. L.A. didn't invent disparity, but it feels more blatant than anywhere else I've lived.

rabble rabble...

IT'S HARD TO STAY HEALTHY. THERE'S FREE FOOD EVERYWHERE IN THE STUDIO. IT'S EASY TO GAIN WEIGHT. I GET DEPRESSED FROM TIME TO TIME BECAUSE I DON'T WALK MUCH IN L.A. OR GET MUCH NATURE TIME.

THERE'S THIS FEELING OF LIVING IN A BUBBLE, BETWEEN AN AIR-CONDITIONED CAR, AN AIR-CONDITIONED OFFICE, AND AN AIR-CONDITIONED APARTMENT.

Not that I want to give up the A.C.

IT'S A SYMPTOM OF DRIVING EVERYWHERE, AND IT'S NOT UNIQUE TO L.A. BUT...I DON'T STUMBLE ONTO COOL NEW THINGS OR GET TO KNOW MY NEIGHBORHOOD, AND THAT SUCKS.

I MISS **NATURE**. I HAVE TO MAKE A SIZABLE EFFORT TO WALK ON GRASS OR BE SURROUNDED BY TREES HERE.

HIKE

I MISS WALKING. A LOT. I DAYDREAM ABOUT WALKING CITIES ALL OF THE TIME.

409 9/10

AND I MISS **DRAWING** PEOPLE WALKING. I BARELY SKETCH FROM LIFE ANYMORE. IT'S HARD TO FIND A GOOD CAFE WITH SEATING AND A VIEW OF FOOT TRAFFIC LIKE I'M USED TO IN OTHER BIG CITIES. L.A. IS JUST **NOT** A PEDESTRIAN CITY, AND PEOPLE-WATCHING SPOTS ARE FEW AND FAR BETWEEN.

Santa Monica, Muscle Beach, The Grove, L.A. Zoo, Disneyland, Hollywood Blvd, Echo Park, and the Fashion District are O.K. spots.

T.V. AND FEATURE ANIMATION ARE CONSIDERED TO BE TWO PRETTY DIFFERENT THINGS. JUST BECAUSE I HAVE EXPERIENCE BOARDING FOR FEATURE, THAT DOESN'T MEAN I CAN AUTOMATICALLY FIND WORK IN T.V., AND VICE-VERSA. ALSO, I GET THE FEELING THAT FEATURE IS...OLDER? EVERYBODY HERE IS MARRIED! WHEN I LOOK AT T.V., SOMETIMES IT SEEMS LIKE A COLLEGE PARTY BY COMPARISON.

T.V. STORYBOARD ARTISTS OFTEN GET (UNPAID) BREAKS BETWEEN EPISODES OR SEASONS. A LOT OF PEOPLE USE THE BREAK TO TRAVEL OR REST OR MAKE A PERSONAL PROJECT.

IN FEATURE, THE WHOLE MOVIE GETS BOARDED MANY TIMES. EVERY 3 MONTHS OR SO, A TEAM OF STORY ARTISTS BOARDS THE WHOLE MOVIE, SCREENS IT INTERNALLY, AND THEN THROWS MOST OF IT OUT AND DOES IT AGAIN. IT'S GOOD TO LOVE OUR SCENES AND BOARD THEM WITH ALL OF OUR HEARTS, BUT IT'S ALSO WISE TO REMEMBER THAT MOST OF WHAT WE BOARD GETS COMPLETELY SCRAPPED. THAT'S PART OF THE PROCESS.

AT A LOT OF THE STUDIOS, THE ASSUMPTION IS THAT STORY ARTISTS WILL DO WHATEVER THEY HAVE TO DO TO MEET THEIR DEADLINES...EVEN IF THEY GET HANDED AN ASSIGNMENT ON FRIDAY AFTERNOON AND THEY HAVE TO PITCH IT ON MONDAY. IF THERE'S A DEADLINE, OR A LAST-MINUTE CHANGE, OR IT'S CRUNCH TIME, IT'S POSSIBLE TO WORK 50, 55, OR 60-HOUR WEEKS. PERSONALLY, I DON'T HAVE KIDS AND I LIKE THE OVERTIME MONEY, SO I DON'T REALLY MIND AT THIS POINT IN MY LIFE.

Sorry to ask you to work on a Saturday...

It's really no trouble!

WOO-HOO! 1.5 x pay!

PEOPLE ARE LOYAL TO PEOPLE, NOT COMPANIES. I WAS PLEASANTLY SURPRISED AT A HOUSE PARTY WHEN I WAS NEW TO L.A. -- THE GUESTS WERE FROM A BUNCH OF DIFFERENT STUDIOS AND IT DIDN'T MATTER. THEY WERE FRIENDS WHO HAD WORKED TOGETHER AT SOME POINT, NEVERMIND WHAT STUDIO THEY CURRENTLY WORKED FOR.

TO THAT POINT : THIS IS NOT A PLACE TO BURN BRIDGES!!! IT'S A RELATIVELY SMALL INDUSTRY, AND PEOPLE TALK ABOUT PEOPLE WHO'VE BEEN NIGHTMARES TO WORK WITH.

pss pss psst pst pst Whaaat! pst psst

L.A. SOCIAL LIFE : GET USED TO BEING ALONE

THERE ARE SO MANY ARTISTS HERE!

BUT...WHEN IS THE PART WHERE WE HANG OUT?

PEOPLE FLAKE A **LOT**. I'VE STARTED TO DO IT, TOO. IT'S A COMBINATION OF GEOGRAPHY AND THE FACT THAT IT'S MORE CULTURALLY ACCEPTABLE HERE TO CANCEL LAST-MINUTE. IF I'M TRYING TO WATCH A MOVIE WITH 5 PEOPLE, I INVITE 10.

I'm tired. ☹ Rain check?

NO what the hell!

IT'S REALLY HARD TO GET A BIG GROUP OF PEOPLE IN ONE SPOT. I'M USED TO HANGING OUT WITH A BIG GROUP OF FRIENDS ON THE REGULAR, MAKING LAST-MINUTE PLANS AND MEETING AT SOME PUB THAT'S CLOSE TO EVERYONE. IN L.A., PEOPLE DON'T WANT TO DRIVE 30 MINUTES TO SEE ME AFTER WORK. MOST PEOPLE RUN HOME AND STAY THERE.

Beer?

...K, bye.

IT FEELS LIKE I'M ALWAYS FIGHTING GEOGRAPHY IN L.A. THE CITY IS **SO** DECENTRALIZED. MY ERRANDS ARE OFTEN 15 MINUTES APART FROM EACH OTHER, NOT IN ONE "DOWNTOWN" AREA. MOST PEOPLE GET AROUND IN CARS, MOST TRIPS REQUIRE A CAR, AND WALKING AND BIKING FEEL UNSAFE AND UNCOMFORTABLE.

I'VE HAD MORE SUCCESS MEETING PEOPLE ON THE WEEKENDS, ESPECIALLY FOR HIKING, DISNEYLAND, AND BEACH TRIPS.

I'M NOT USUALLY PRONE TO LONELINESS, BUT I FELT IT A **LOT** MY FIRST YEAR IN L.A. I TRIED LIVING ALONE FOR THE FIRST TIME, AND IN HINDSIGHT THAT WAS STUPID. I DIDN'T KNOW ALMOST ANYONE!

THIS CONVERSATION WITH A FRIEND WHO ALSO MOVED FROM THE PORTLAND AREA PRETTY MUCH SUMS UP HOW I FELT ABOUT THE CITY ITSELF WHEN I WAS NEW HERE :

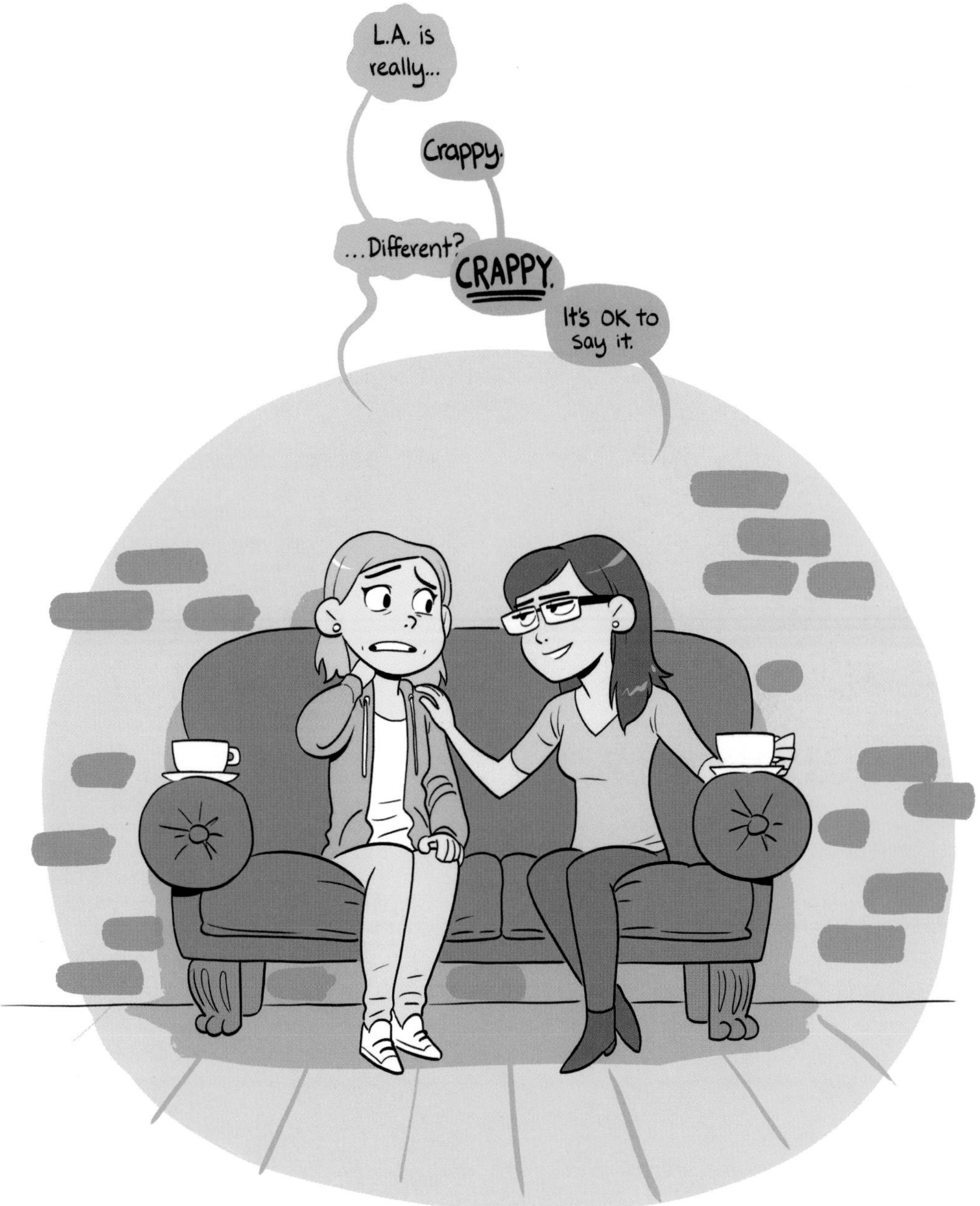

L.A. is really...
Crappy.
...Different?
CRAPPY.
It's OK to say it.

How to Break in

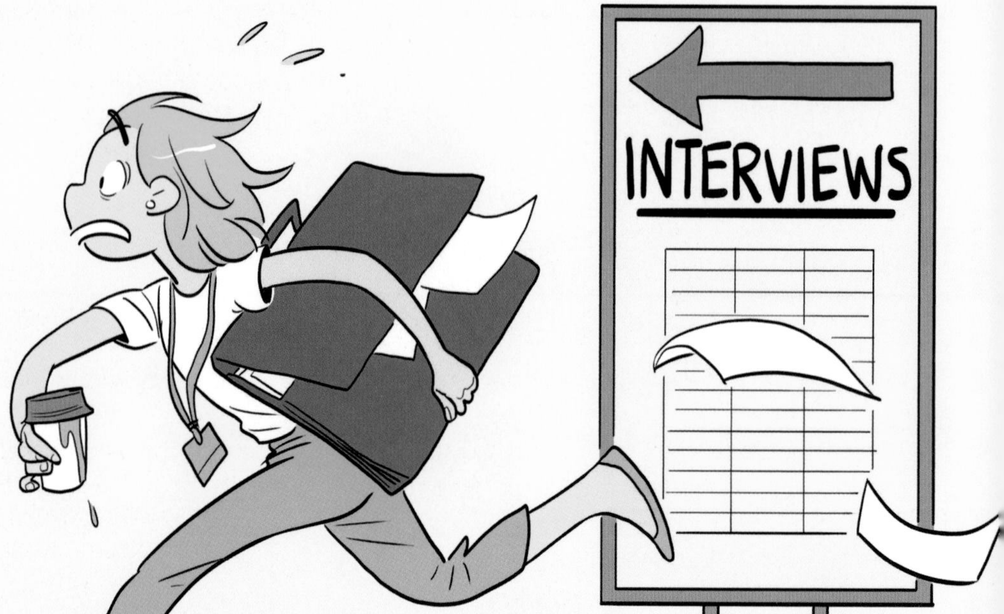
INTERVIEWS

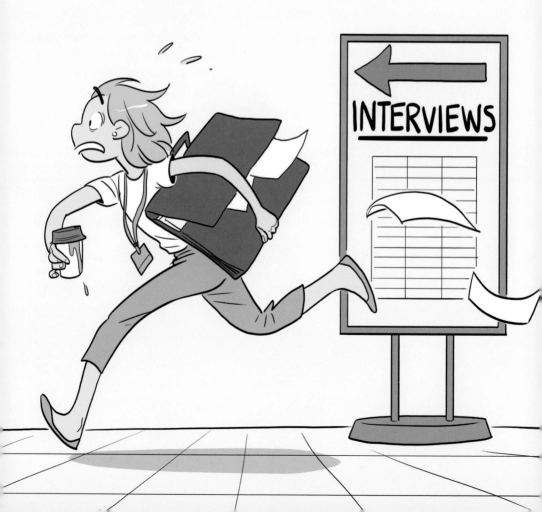

"HOW DO I GET MY FIRST JOB IN AN ANIMATION STUDIO?"

Oh god. This is the question I get the most, and it's the one I feel the least qualified to answer.

I'm still going to give an answer, because anything is better than a shrug and a "good luck".

BUT – I am not a recruiter, I do not speak for any studio, every studio is different, what studios look for changes over time, and I believe a lot of it comes down to luck and timing.

First: **APPLY.** Apply to lots of jobs at lots of studios. Apply at big, Guild studios and small, non-Guild studios. Apply to new job postings at the same studios over and over and over again. That's not annoying or pathetic – that's persistent.

You can't get a job you don't apply for, so start applying, even if you don't think you're ready yet. Even if you don't get the job, it's good practice putting yourself out there and prepping a portfolio!

Studio Z   Studio Y   Studio X

Heads it's Miranda, tails it's Shiroy.

GETTING TURNED DOWN FOR A JOB DOES **NOT** REFLECT POORLY ON YOU. IT DOESN'T MEAN YOU WOULDN'T GET THE JOB ON A DIFFERENT DAY. THERE IS SO MUCH HAPPENING INTERNALLY AT STUDIOS THAT YOU HAVE NO CONTROL OVER, PLEASE DON'T TAKE IT PERSONALLY WHEN YOU GET TURNED DOWN. JUST MOVE ON TO THE NEXT JOB LISTING.

JOB POSTINGS LIST ALL OF THE TRAITS OF AN **IDEAL** CANDIDATE, BUT THEY WILL TAKE THE **BEST** CANDIDATE THEY GET. SO EVEN IF YOU DON'T MEET ALL OF THEIR CRITERIA, YOU SHOULD STILL APPLY!

...OR ELSE SOMEONE LESS QUALIFIED MIGHT GET THE JOB BECAUSE THEY HAD THE GUTS TO APPLY!

My first job was listed as a position for "candidates less than 5 years out of school". I was 6 years out of school, so I normally would have counted myself out of the running automatically and not taken the time to apply.

I only applied because I was encouraged to by a recruiter. Then I got the job! To think, I would have been my own worst enemy and missed the opportunity, just for trying to follow the rules!

On another note... Please don't be too harsh on yourself about your drawing skills.

I'm surprised how much of this job is not even about drawing. Equally vital are: original ideas, knowing how to give and take constructive criticism, humility, reliability, speed, a collaborative attitude, clear communication, story structure, film theory, etc.

Which is good, because, look... I can draw O.K., but I'm no Claire Wendling...feel me?

IN HINDSIGHT, MY BIG BREAKS CAME FROM...

1 FRIENDS!

MADDY INVITED ME TO FREELANCE BOARD AN EPISODE OF *BEE & PUPPYCAT* WITH HER. THAT WAS MY FIRST EXPERIENCE STORY-BOARDING FOR ANIMATION, AND SOMETHING CONCRETE TO PUT ON MY RESUME.

2 STORYBOARDING

THE BEST WAY TO GET STORYBOARDING WORK IS TO HAVE STORYBOARD SAMPLES IN YOUR PORTFOLIO. IT SOUNDS OBVIOUS, BUT YOU'D BE SURPRISED HOW MANY PEOPLE APPLY TO STORY POSITIONS WITHOUT STORYBOARDS TO SHOW. YOU DON'T NEED A STORYBOARDING JOB TO MAKE STORYBOARD SAMPLES! THE BEST ADVICE I GOT FROM A PRO WHILE I WAS JOB-HUNTING WAS TO STORYBOARD MY OWN SHORT STORY, PUT IT ONLINE, AND THEN DO IT AGAIN. THAT WAS SUCH A FAST WAY TO IMPROVE, GET EYES ON MY WORK, AND BUILD SAMPLES FOR MY PORTFOLIO. I DIDN'T KNOW WHAT I WAS DOING AT **ALL** AT FIRST, BUT THAT'S OK - THINGS GOT EASIER WITH EACH SHORT STORY I BOARDED.

3 MAKING NEW ART AND PUTTING IT ONLINE

I ANIMATED A 12-SECOND SHORT FOR LOOPDELOOP, JUST AS AN EXCUSE TO LEARN HOW THE ANIMATION PIPELINE WORKED AND TRY TO GET SOMETHING ANIMATED IN MY PORTFOLIO. ONE OF THE LOOPDELOOP ORGANIZERS KEPT IN CONTACT AND GAVE ME STORY TESTS AT THE STUDIO WHERE SHE WORKED. (YOU'LL MEET HER LATER!)

4 IN-PERSON NETWORKING

I JOINED ASIFA'S PORTLAND BRANCH AND WENT TO DRINK N' DRAWS AND SCREENINGS, AND MET REALLY SWEET AND PASSIONATE ARTISTS. WE SHARED RESOURCES AND POSTED ON FACEBOOK WHENEVER A COMPANY WAS HIRING, TO HELP EACH OTHER OUT.

5 INSTAGRAM AND...LINKEDIN?!

A DIRECTOR SAW MY WORK ON INSTAGRAM AND CONTACTED ME ON LINKEDIN ABOUT AN OPEN STORY ARTIST POSITION. I RECOMMEND TO EVERY ASPIRING STORY ARTIST TO MAINTAIN THEIR SOCIAL MEDIA PROFILES AND UPLOAD NEW ARTWORK TO THEM REGULARLY.

This... CANNOT be true.

Believe it!!

EVEN THOUGH YOU CAN MEET PEOPLE, TAKE CLASSES, AND APPLY TO JOBS ONLINE...
I REALLY BELIEVE IN THE POWER OF MEETING PEOPLE FACE-TO-FACE. IT'S NOT FAIR,
BUT I BELIEVE IT'S A REALITY AND I WANT TO BE HONEST ABOUT THAT.

EXAMPLE : SDCC 2013. I'M 25, I HAVE HAD **ZERO** LUCK APPLYING TO JOBS ONLINE, AND I'M GOING TO FRANCE NEXT MONTH TO WORK AS AN AU PAIR.

I'M HANDING OUT MINICOMICS OF MY WORK ANYWAY TO NETWORK FOR THE FUTURE.

2013 Sketchbook
Natalie Nourigat

IT'S THE LAST NIGHT OF THE CON. I GO OUT WITHOUT PLANS AND FIND MYSELF AT A BAR WHERE I KNOW NO ONE.

This is my nightmare.

I DECIDE TO PLAY THIS GAME I PLAY WHEN I FEEL SOCIALLY ANXIOUS : I HAVE TO INTRODUCE MYSELF TO **ONE** NEW PERSON, AND THEN WHEN THE CONVERSATION ENDS I'M ALLOWED TO GO HOME.

Hiiiiiiii!

Awkward as hell

SOMEHOW, I FUMBLE MY WAY INTO A NICE CONVERSATION.

Do you know anyone here?

Yeah, we all work on the same TV show.

Really?? I'm trying to become a board artist.

Oh, this is good.

Thanks!

2 HOURS LATER:

Don't go to France! Come work on our show! This is our showrunner!

This is good! Are you available?

S-seriously?

Seriously.

WHAAAA

AUGH, why is this happening **NOW**?!

BECAUSE COMIC CON.

SOME STUDIOS HAVE INTERNSHIPS OR INTERMEDIARY TRAINING POSITIONS (LIKE AN "APPRENTICE" OR "TRAINEE").

I would put the camera lower here, eye-level with your character, so we're more in her head.

NOD

THEY TEND TO PAY LESS THAN A FULL "JOURNEYMAN" POSITION, BUT THE EXPECTATIONS ARE ALSO LOWER, SO AN ARTIST IS ALLOWED TO MAKE MISTAKES AND LEARN ON THE JOB. IT'S POSSIBLE TO GET HIRED AS A STORY ARTIST AFTER COMPLETING TRAINING PROGRAMS, BUT SHOULDN'T BE EXPECTED.

KNOWING SOMEONE IN A STUDIO CAN MAKE A BIG DIFFERENCE. PUT THE WORD OUT TO YOUR FRIENDS THAT YOU ARE LOOKING FOR WORK. MAYBE THEY KNOW SOMEONE THEY CAN INTRODUCE YOU TO.

gulp!

Suzy A

Hey y'all, I'm looking for a storyboard artist position in animation, if anybody knows of an open position! Here's a link to my portfolio: goo.gl/j78vu3gl

IF YOU MEET SOMEONE IN A STUDIO, OFFER TO BUY THEM LUNCH OR COFFEE. ASK THEM ABOUT THEIR CAREER JOURNEY, AND TELL THEM A BIT ABOUT YOUR JOB SEARCH.

I'd love to hear how you got to where you are, and if you have any advice to an artist looking for their first studio position.

GET OUT TO ANIMATION EVENTS AND MEET PEOPLE. HAND OUT YOUR BUSINESS CARD.

BUT...TRY NOT TO COME ON TOO HARD OR APPEAR "HUNGRY" (EVEN IF YOU ARE). DESPERATION SCARES PEOPLE AWAY.

PLEASE look at my work, I really need a job!!!!

WHEN YOU GET GIGS, NO MATTER HOW SMALL OR FAR FROM ANIMATION, DO THE BEST WORK YOU CAN AND BE PROFESSIONAL. WORD OF MOUTH IS INVALUABLE, AND JOBS HAVE A WAY OF LEADING TO BETTER JOBS IF YOUR CLIENT IS HAPPY WORKING WITH YOU.

EVERYBODY KNOWS EVERYBODY - IF YOU'RE DOING FREELANCE BOARDS FOR A CLIENT AND YOU MENTION THAT YOU'RE TRYING TO FIND A FULL-TIME GIG IN L.A., THEY MIGHT KNOW SOMEBODY.

Thanks for the great work this week on those illustrations. You mentioned that you are seeking a position in animation, and I remembered I have a friend at (studio). Want me to make an introduction?

AS FOR A PORTFOLIO, READ JOB POSTINGS FOR THE POSITION YOU WANT CLOSELY. EXAMINE YOUR OWN PORTFOLIO / WEBSITE AS IF YOU WERE THE RECRUITER FOR THAT JOB. DO YOU HAVE THE KIND OF SAMPLES THEY ARE ASKING FOR? IF YOU WANT SOME EXERCISES TO TRY, HERE ARE A FEW I RECOMMEND :

KEEP A JOURNAL! IT'S A SAFE SPACE TO WRITE AND DEVELOP YOUR VOICE AND YOUR OPINIONS.	DRAW COMICS! I AM A HUGE BELIEVER IN MAKING COMICS AS A WAY TO BUILD DRAWING & NARRATIVE SKILLS.	DRAW THE THINGS YOU SEE AROUND YOU. TRAIN YOURSELF TO BE OBSERVANT AND PICK UP ON DETAILS FROM THE REAL WORLD.

STORYBOARD YOUR OWN SHORT STORY IDEAS

Hmm...I have those 2 vampire characters... what if I board their first encounter?

REVERSE-STORYBOARD : WATCH A MOVIE SCENE YOU LIKE OVER AND OVER, AND THEN STORYBOARD IT.

DRAW STORY MOMENTS : CLEAR, SIMPLE ILLUSTRA- TIONS THAT TELL A STORY WITH A STRONG EMOTION. THEY CAN COME FROM YOUR IMAGINATION.....

...OR FROM SOMETHING YOU SAW WHILE SKETCHING THE WORLD. IT'S OK TO EMBELISH!

The number one thing I would put in a story portfolio, besides storyboard samples, is cartoony/embellished sketches from life.

LIKE, GET IN THE HABIT OF SITTING IN A CAFE OR MALL OR ON THE BEACH FOR 2 HOURS AND DRAWING THE HUMAN THINGS THAT YOU SEE. NOT DRAWING THINGS EXACTLY AS THEY **ARE**....BUT HOW **YOU** PERSONALLY SEE THEM. USE "LIES" TO TELL THE TRUTH. EXAGGERATE HUMAN DETAILS / INTERACTIONS / GESTURES / FUNNY PROPORTIONS / FUNNY SITUATIONS. THAT'S SO HELPFUL FOR RECRUITERS, WHO ARE LOOKING FOR ARTISTS WITH UNIQUE VOICES, PERSONALITIES, OPINIONS, AND SENSES OF HUMOR.

EXPRESSION SHEETS : DRAW ONE CHARACTER OVER AND OVER WITH EVERY DIFFERENT EXPRESSION YOU CAN THINK OF. LEARN TO DRAW A CHARACTER THAT'S RECOGNIZABLE FROM DIFFERENT ANGLES AND WITH DIFFERENT EXPRESSIONS.

SHAPE EXERCISE : DRAW A BUNCH OF BIG, FUNKY SHAPES, THEN GO BACK WITH A PEN AND TURN THEM INTO FACES OR BODIES OR CREATURES

SUBMIT A SHORT FILM TO LOOPDELOOP!

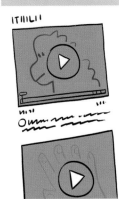

Good luck...!

Other FAQ

Other F.A.Q.

"DO I HAVE TO DRAW IN A STUDIO'S 'HOUSE STYLE'?"

Not in my experience, especially in feature. As long as people can recognize which character is which, different story artists draw in their own styles.

Artist A   Artist B   Artist C

IN T.V. I THINK IT'S MORE IMPORTANT, ESPECIALLY IF EPISODES ARE BEING SENT OVERSEAS FOR ANIMATION. IN THAT CASE, IT MIGHT BE REALLY IMPORTANT TO DRAW CHARACTERS ON-MODEL.

"WHERE CAN I NETWORK / MEET PEOPLE?"

Go to events at Center Stage Gallery, Gallery Nucleus, W.I.A., any industry events you can, CTNX, and L.A. Film Festivals or screenings of animation...

LIFE DRAWING AT CENTER STAGE, TITMOUSE, GARAGE MAHAL, AND POP SECRET...

COMIC CONVENTIONS LIKE CALA, SDCC, AND THE L.A. ZINE FEST...

...AND CLASSES AT T.A.G., SILA, AND CDA!

Other F.A.Q.

"WHAT SOFTWARE DO STUDIOS USE FOR BOARDING?"

Most studios use Photoshop, T.V. Paint, or Storyboard Pro. They may also use their own software, which they can train you to use.

"WHAT IF I DON'T HAVE A COMPUTER / A TABLET / PHOTOSHOP?"

I won't lie — most studios want you to be comfortable drawing digitally.

LOOK FOR ANY OPPORTUNITY TO USE DRAWING SOFTWARE AND TABLETS OR CINTIQS – ASK ABOUT IT AT YOUR SCHOOL AND LOCAL LIBRARY.

BUT DON'T DISMAY IF YOU DON'T HAVE THE TECH YET - PIXAR STORY INTERNS DRAW ON SCRAP PAPER WITH SHARPIES AND PENCILS, BECAUSE THE FUNDAMENTALS OF STORYBOARDING / STORYTELLING HAVE NOTHING TO DO WITH WHAT TECHNOLOGY YOU HAVE ACCESS TO OR THE BRUSHES / PENS YOU USE.

Bill Peet didn't have a Cintiq!

USE WHATEVER TOOLS YOU HAVE TO PRACTICE, STORYBOARD, AND BUILD A PORTFOLIO! EVEN SCRAP PAPER AND SHARPIES!

Some of the most talented board artists I know draw with ballpoint pens!

"DO I NEED TO KNOW FILM VOCABULARY?"

IT DOES NOT HURT! BUT I LEARNED MOST OF THIS ON THE JOB.

Can we get this shot in C.U.?*

Y...yes.

Ga gle

what is "cu" in film?

*CLOSE-UP

Other F.A.Q.

"SHOULD I MOVE TO L.A. IF I DON'T HAVE A JOB YET...?"

I'VE HEARD FROM MULTIPLE PEOPLE THAT IT'S AN ADVANTAGE TO ALREADY BE IN THE CITY, THAT RECRUITERS TAKE YOUR APPLICATION MORE SERIOUSLY. ALSO, SINCE SO MANY STUDIO JOBS ARE IN L.A., MOST OF THE ARTISTS YOU'D WANT TO NETWORK WITH AND ASK FOR ADVICE ARE HERE, TOO.

Great question.

Move first! You'll find a job faster. Just save a little $ and do it.

THE RISK OF MOVING WITHOUT A JOB IS SOMETHING YOU HAVE TO DETERMINE FOR YOURSELF.

I can't risk losing my savings and having to move back home...

I don't want to start over from 0 again.

I HELD OUT UNTIL I GOT A JOB FIRST, BECAUSE I WAS SCARED OF BURNING THROUGH MY SAVINGS. I THINK THAT WAS THE RIGHT CHOICE FOR ME, BECAUSE IT TOOK ME MORE THAN A YEAR TO LAND MY JOB.

It also meant I got a **RELOCATION BONUS!**

I'll be Captain Obvious and say: if you're moving to L.A. without a job, **save up AS MUCH MONEY** as you possibly can first. It will disappear quickly.

IF YOU DECIDE TO STAY AT HOME AND WAIT IT OUT LIKE I DID, YOU CAN STILL NETWORK WITH L.A. ANIMATION FOLKS FROM AFAR! POST NEW ART TO SOCIAL MEDIA, COMMENT ON OTHERS' ART, FOLLOW PEOPLE WORKING IN YOUR FIELD, TAKE ONLINE CLASSES FROM WORKING PROS, AND BUILD PROFESSIONAL FRIENDSHIPS BIT BY BIT. GO TO ANIMATION CONVENTIONS OR EVENTS IF AT ALL POSSIBLE. ANIMATION IS A RELATIVELY SMALL, FRIENDLY COMMUNITY, SO ONE FRIEND CAN QUICKLY TURN INTO MANY FRIENDS.

@Starryskye00 I love your character designs!

@Kaylartaccount Thanks! I like your stuff, too!

Other F.A.Q.

"CAN I KEEP WORKING ON MY OWN PROJECTS?"

That's my experience so far.

I finished a 96-page graphic novel during my first year story-boarding. That wasn't a **FUN** schedule, but it's possible.

MOST OF THE CARTOONISTS I KNOW STORYBOARD DURING THE DAY AND WORK ON THEIR COMICS AT NIGHT, WITH NO INTERFERENCE FROM THEIR EMPLOYERS. IT'S MORE LIKELY TO BE A CONFLICT OF INTEREST IF YOU'RE WORKING ON A FILM OR FREELANCING FOR ANOTHER STUDIO.*

*TALK TO YOUR EMPLOYER TO BE SURE

"IS ANIMATION A STRAIGHT / WHITE / BOYS' CLUB?"

Hmm.

I'm really happy that the story rooms I've been in so far have been half women, and there's a lot of respect for women's voices. I'm really happy I work with openly gay people and not....**ALL** white people.

There are women and LGBTQ people and P.O.C. in high positions. I feel supported now that I'm here.

But...let's just say there is always room for improvement.

PLEASE just use that as inspiration to apply if you are not a straight, white, cis male.

YOUR VOICE IS NEEDED IN THE ROOM!

I think that recruiters and directors understand that.

Other F.A.Q.

"WHAT...AHEM...**INCOME** CAN I EXPECT FROM AN ANIMATION STUDIO JOB?"

To generalize...at Guild studios, the minimum wage* is set pretty high. A full-time story artist position pays over $45/hour.

If you work 40 hours per week, 50 weeks per year at that rate, you'd make $90,000 per year.

*CHECK THE CONTRACT WAGE PDFS ON T.A.G.'S WEBSITE FOR THE MOST CURRENT INFORMATION ON THE MINIMUM WAGE FOR THE POSITION YOU WANT AT THE STUDIO YOU WANT.

"DO I HAVE TO BUY BUSINESS CLOTHES TO WORK IN A STUDIO?"

IN ONE OF MY FIRST MEETINGS, I LOOKED AROUND AND SAW THAT EVERY SINGLE PERSON WAS WEARING A CREW T-SHIRT, JEANS, AND CONVERSE SNEAKERS.

Nah.

It's cool.

"DO YOU GET A LOT OF VACATION TIME?"

Depends on who you ask.

I'd like more, of course.

IF I TELL MY FRENCH FRIENDS THAT I GET 2 WEEKS/YEAR:

WHAT? 2 WEEKS?! Is that LEGAL?!?

NOD

IF I TELL OTHER ANIMATION INDUSTRY FRIENDS THAT I GET 2 WEEKS/YEAR:

Lucky! I only get major holidays off from work.

Oh, yikes... I AM lucky....

Other F.A.Q.

"ARE THE OTHER ARTISTS...NICE?"

I KIND OF THOUGHT PEOPLE WOULD BE MORE COMPETITIVE OR...HAUGHTY? BUT THE STORY ARTISTS I'VE MET ARE REALLY HUMBLE AND HAPPY TO HELP OTHER PEOPLE.

The ones I've met are!

I THINK WE ALL HAD A LOT OF HELP GETTING HERE, AND WE KNOW WE'RE SUPPOSED TO PAY THAT FORWARD. STORYBOARDING IS ALSO COLLABORATIVE BY NATURE. WE EDIT EACH OTHER'S SCENES ALL OF THE TIME, SO THERE'S NOT A LOT OF ROOM FOR EGO. "ALL STORY, NO GLORY", THEY SAY!

WHEN I ASK MY COWORKERS FOR HELP, THEY DROP WHAT THEY'RE DOING TO COME LOOK AT MY BOARDS AND MAKE SUGGESTIONS OR SHOW ME PHOTOSHOP SHORTCUTS.

"AM I TOO OLD TO GET INTO THE ANIMATION INDUSTRY?"

I don't think age matters.

Studios want the best talent, whatever age it comes in. These jobs don't usually last very long, so as long as you're good to work for another few years, I don't think it matters if you're not 22 anymore.

Other F.A.Q.

"WAIT. ARE YOU SAYING I'LL NEED TO JOB SEARCH AGAIN EVERY FEW YEARS??"

Well, from what I've observed, story artists change jobs a **LOT**. Way more than I expected.

Especially my friends in T.V. animation. They change jobs every 1 or 2 years.

EAMWORKS TV

CARTOON NE

ICKELODEON

IF THEY GET LET GO OR THEIR SHOW IS CANCELLED, THEY NORMALLY AREN'T UNEMPLOYED FOR LONG. THERE'S ALWAYS SOME SHOW STARTING UP THAT NEEDS PEOPLE.

MOST VETERAN STORY ARTISTS HAVE LONG LISTS OF STUDIOS THEY'VE WORKED FOR.

THEY EVEN GET POACHED WHILE THEY'RE STILL ON ANOTHER SHOW!

AND NOT TO BE A DOWNER, BUT... STUDIOS SHUT DOWN, MASSIVE LAYOFFS HAPPEN. TECHNOLOGY CHANGES. THE INDUSTRY EVOLVES. THOSE ARE DEFINITELY OCCUPATIONAL HAZARDS.

SO NO, THESE JOBS DON'T LAST FOREVER. IT'S A GOOD IDEA TO KEEP NETWORKING EVEN AFTER YOU LAND A GOOD POSITION, SAVE YOUR MONEY, AND TRY TO HAVE A BACK-UP PLAN.

That said, I know some artists who have been at the same studio for 20+ years. It can happen!

"DO I NEED TO GO TO ART SCHOOL TO WORK IN ANIMATION?"

No.

"DO I NEED TO KNOW HOW TO ANIMATE OR HAVE A REEL TO GET A STORY ARTIST JOB?"

No.

"DO I NEED A WESTSIDE RENTALS ACCOUNT?"

NO!!

"WHAT'S IT LIKE CHANGING FOCUS FROM A COMICS CAREER TO ANIMATION?"

I like being a part of a team, and working with other people who are passionate about making the best movie/episode possible.

...But I miss having total ownership and creative freedom, so I keep making comics in my free time to get that.

ONE OF THE HARDEST THINGS WHEN I TRANSITIONED WAS LEARNING TO DRAW MORE LOOSELY, AND TO BE OK WITH TURNING IN UNFINISHED ARTWORK. COMING FROM COMICS, WHERE EVERYTHING IS DRAWN 2-3 TIMES AND THE LINES LOOK CLEAN, IT FELT SOOOOO WRONG TO TURN IN SKETCHY STORYBOARD DRAWINGS.

UGHHH... these boards are so ugly and rough...! He's going to think I'm lazy! Or that I don't know how to draw...!

These are reeeally polished... It looks too stiff. Try to loosen up.

Other F.A.Q.

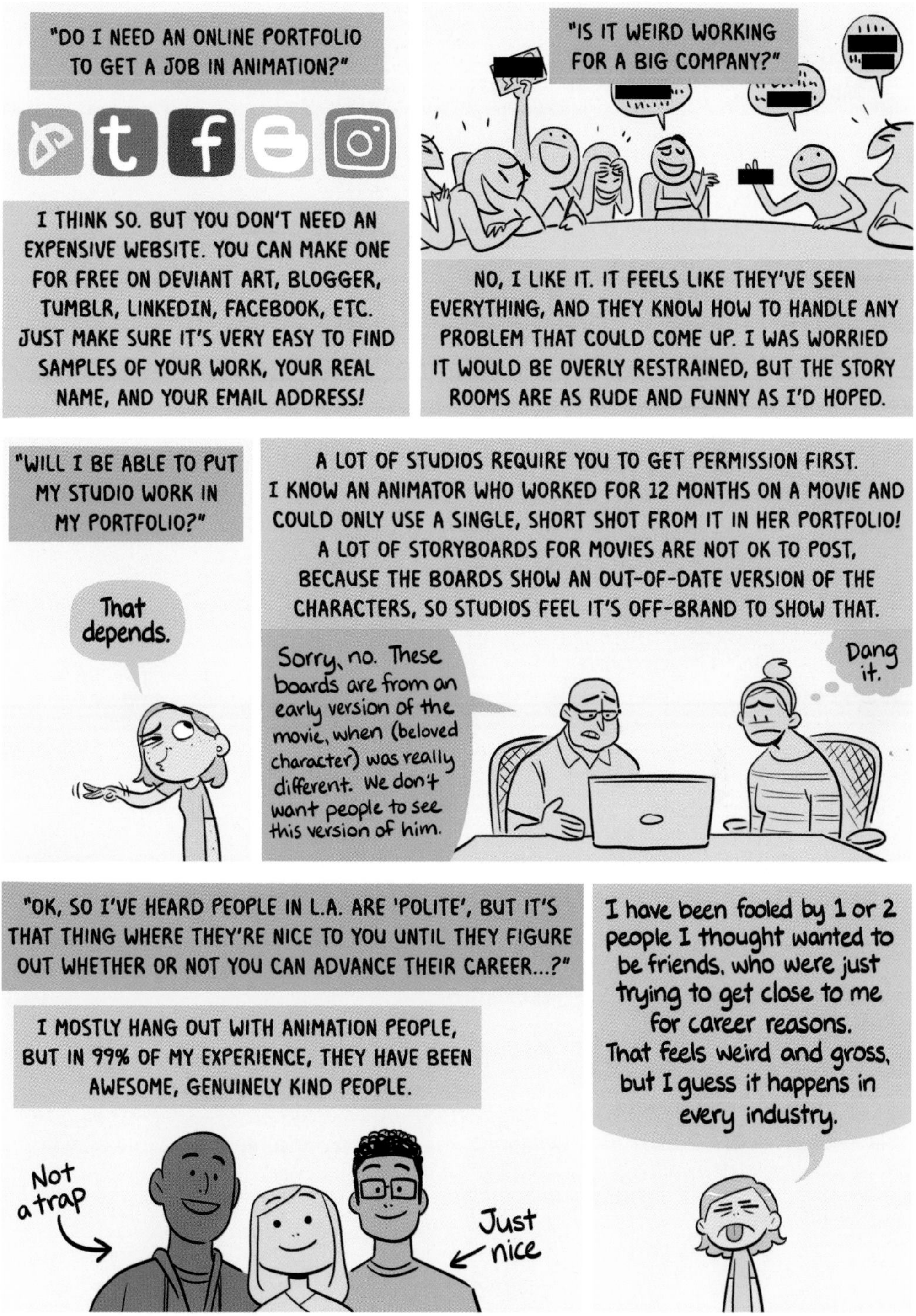
"DO I NEED AN ONLINE PORTFOLIO TO GET A JOB IN ANIMATION?"
I THINK SO. BUT YOU DON'T NEED AN EXPENSIVE WEBSITE. YOU CAN MAKE ONE FOR FREE ON DEVIANT ART, BLOGGER, TUMBLR, LINKEDIN, FACEBOOK, ETC. JUST MAKE SURE IT'S VERY EASY TO FIND SAMPLES OF YOUR WORK, YOUR REAL NAME, AND YOUR EMAIL ADDRESS!
"IS IT WEIRD WORKING FOR A BIG COMPANY?"
[redacted]
[redacted]
[redacted]
[redacted]
[redacted]
NO, I LIKE IT. IT FEELS LIKE THEY'VE SEEN EVERYTHING, AND THEY KNOW HOW TO HANDLE ANY PROBLEM THAT COULD COME UP. I WAS WORRIED IT WOULD BE OVERLY RESTRAINED, BUT THE STORY ROOMS ARE AS RUDE AND FUNNY AS I'D HOPED.
"WILL I BE ABLE TO PUT MY STUDIO WORK IN MY PORTFOLIO?"
That depends.
A LOT OF STUDIOS REQUIRE YOU TO GET PERMISSION FIRST. I KNOW AN ANIMATOR WHO WORKED FOR 12 MONTHS ON A MOVIE AND COULD ONLY USE A SINGLE, SHORT SHOT FROM IT IN HER PORTFOLIO! A LOT OF STORYBOARDS FOR MOVIES ARE NOT OK TO POST, BECAUSE THE BOARDS SHOW AN OUT-OF-DATE VERSION OF THE CHARACTERS, SO STUDIOS FEEL IT'S OFF-BRAND TO SHOW THAT.
Sorry, no. These boards are from an early version of the movie, when (beloved character) was really different. We don't want people to see this version of him.
Dang it.
"OK, SO I'VE HEARD PEOPLE IN L.A. ARE 'POLITE', BUT IT'S THAT THING WHERE THEY'RE NICE TO YOU UNTIL THEY FIGURE OUT WHETHER OR NOT YOU CAN ADVANCE THEIR CAREER...?"
I MOSTLY HANG OUT WITH ANIMATION PEOPLE, BUT IN 99% OF MY EXPERIENCE, THEY HAVE BEEN AWESOME, GENUINELY KIND PEOPLE.
Not a trap
Just nice
I have been fooled by 1 or 2 people I thought wanted to be friends, who were just trying to get close to me for career reasons. That feels weird and gross, but I guess it happens in every industry.

Other F.A.Q.

"IS THERE UPWARD MOBILITY FOR STORY-BOARD ARTISTS?"

I guess?

A LOT OF FEATURE DIRECTORS WERE ONCE STORYBOARD ARTISTS. IN T.V., I GUESS YOU COULD PITCH YOUR OWN SHOW OR BECOME A DIRECTOR. SOME STUDIOS HAVE INTERMEDIARY POSITIONS LIKE "HEAD OF STORY" OR "STORY DIRECTOR" REQUIRING, LIKE, 5 YEARS OF EXPERIENCE AS A STORY ARTIST.

Directors

Heads of Story

Story Artists

A LOT OF PEOPLE WANT TO BE DIRECTORS, AND DIRECTORS HOLD ONTO THEIR POSITIONS FOR A LONG TIME, SO IT SHOULDN'T BE EXPECTED.

I WANT TO BE A DIRECTOR, SO IT SURPRISED ME TO MEET PEOPLE WHO HAVE BEEN STORY ARTISTS FOR 10+ YEARS, LOVE IT, AND INTEND TO DO IT UNTIL THEY RETIRE.

I would have less time with my kids, no thank you.

Nah, I love storyboarding. I don't want a job where I'd draw less.

Can you imagine the stress...?

You couldn't pay me to take on that responsibility! People's jobs rely on you!

I used to be a director. It's not for me — I'm happy to be back in story.

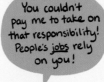

I GET THE IMPRESSION THAT STORY IS ACTUALLY A RELATIVELY STABLE CAREER CHOICE WITHIN ANIMATION...

Story artists are **LUCKY**... Most animators are looking at a life of moving all over the country and the **WORLD** chasing work.

Really??

RECRUITERS TELL ME ALL OF THE TIME THAT THERE'S A SHORTAGE OF GOOD STORY ARTISTS, SO AT LEAST FOR NOW, WE HAVE SOME NEGOTIATING POWER AND OPTIONS BETWEEN THE STUDIOS.

(Showrunner friend) We're still looking for board artists if you know anyone who's available!!!!

Other F.A.Q.

"DO I NEED A FAKE TAN AND FAKE BOOBIES TO FIT IN?"

O.K., so, there **ARE** lots of unnaturally beautiful people...

I chalk it up to the number of pretty, young, aspiring actors flocking to L.A. But it's not like you feel weird if you're a non-enhanced human being. There are plenty of us in L.A., too.

"WHEN WILL THE FAULT LINE OPEN UP AND SWALLOW ME WHOLE?"

Any day now.

"CAN I AVOID DRIVING ON THE HIGHWAYS?"

← Route options
Avoid highways
Avoid tolls
Avoid ferries

FOR SHORT TRIPS YOU CAN USE "SURFACE STREETS" INSTEAD OF HIGHWAYS. GOOGLE MAPS HAS AN "AVOID HIGHWAYS" OPTION.

"AM I GOING TO SPEND 3 HOURS / DAY IN TRAFFIC?"

I REEEEALLY RECOMMEND PAYING MORE AND LIVING CLOSE TO WORK TO AVOID THIS...!

BUT IF YOU HAVE TO ACCEPT A LONG COMMUTE...HEY, THAT'S WHAT PODCASTS AND AUDIOBOOKS ARE FOR!

Stay sexy, don't get murdered!

"PEOPLE DRIVE LIKE LUNATICS, RIGHT? AM I GOING TO DIE?!"

That's... kind of true.

THERE ARE JERKS AND YOU'LL SEE INSANE THINGS ON THE HIGHWAY. PEOPLE DRIVE LIKE THEY ARE IN A BIG HURRY, WEAVE THROUGH TRAFFIC, MANEUVER DANGEROUSLY TO PASS ONE CAR. IT'S THE CULTURE HERE.

IMHO, SAFE DRIVING IN L.A. MEANS ASSIMILATING AND DRIVING THE WAY PEOPLE EXPECT — THAT IS, MORE AGGRESSIVELY.

Other F.A.Q.

WHILE I WAS VISITING MADDY IN L.A. TO SEE IF I COULD LIVE HERE, THE CRAZIEST THING HAPPENED ON THE HIGHWAY.

A MAN RAN ACROSS 8 LANES OF TRAFFIC ON I-5.

HONK HONK

Ohhh crap ...

WE NARROWLY AVOIDED HITTING HIM. HE CAUSED A CRASH RIGHT NEXT TO US, BUT AS FAR AS I KNOW HE MADE IT TO THE OTHER SIDE UNHARMED.

CRASH

Omigod! Omigod! Omigod!

SCREEECH!!!

SO THAT WAS MY FIRST IMPRESSION OF DRIVING IN L.A.!

I guess this is what driving in L.A. is like.

Call the police!

OMG... OMG....

I NEVER SAW THAT SPECIFIC THING AGAIN, BUT I HAVE SEEN CRAZY STUFF WHILE DRIVING AND YOU WILL, TOO.

"WHAT WAS IT LIKE LIVING THERE DURING THE DROUGHT??"

PRIVILEGE

Uhh...the price of almonds went up? And waiters didn't pour me water unless I asked for it? Otherwise...normal.

THE EMERGENCY WATER PROVISIONS WERE CALLED OFF APRIL 7 2017 AFTER RECORD RAINFALL OVER THE WINTER ENDED THE DROUGHT. BUT L.A. IS A DRY AREA NORMALLY, AND IT DOES FEEL UNSUSTAINABLE TO EVEN HAVE SUCH A BIG CITY HERE. ANOTHER DROUGHT COULD HAPPEN ANY TIME.

Other F.A.Q.

"I HEARD THAT THE SMOG IS SO BAD, YOU CAN'T SEE THE MOUNTAINS FROM 5 MILES AWAY."

I've heard from Angelenos that this was 100% true in the 80's and 90's, but new requirements for cars and factories have improved conditions.

I mean, I don't think the black dust that settles on the surfaces near my windows is **GOOD** for me...but the L.A. smog/pollution were oversold to me before I moved here.

"WILL I GET USED TO THE HEAT?"

I have.

Mostly.

IT'S STILL WEIRD TO ME THAT ON REALLY HOT DAYS, WALKING A COUPLE OF MILES IS KIND OF DANGEROUS. I KEEP A BIG SUN HAT IN MY CAR AND I WEAR IT WHEN I GO HIKING OR I'M GOING TO BE OUT-SIDE DURING THE MIDDLE OF THE DAY. I KEEP THE TRUNK OF MY CAR STOCKED WITH LOTS OF BOTTLED WATER AND STRONG SUNSCREEN.

My apartment, the studio, and my car have air conditioning, so it's not too bad.

THAT SAID, THERE IS A LONG LIST OF THINGS THAT HAVE MELTED IN MY CAR :

Sunglasses

Breath mints

Sun hat

Also, chapstick turns into lava, very dangerous:

AHHHHH!

AND...THIS IS KIND OF GROSS... BUT IT'S SO DRY HERE, I USE VASELINE INSTEAD OF BODY LOTION. SOMETIMES I EVEN HAVE TO USE IT ON MY FACE!

It's just..... so dry....

Other F.A.Q.

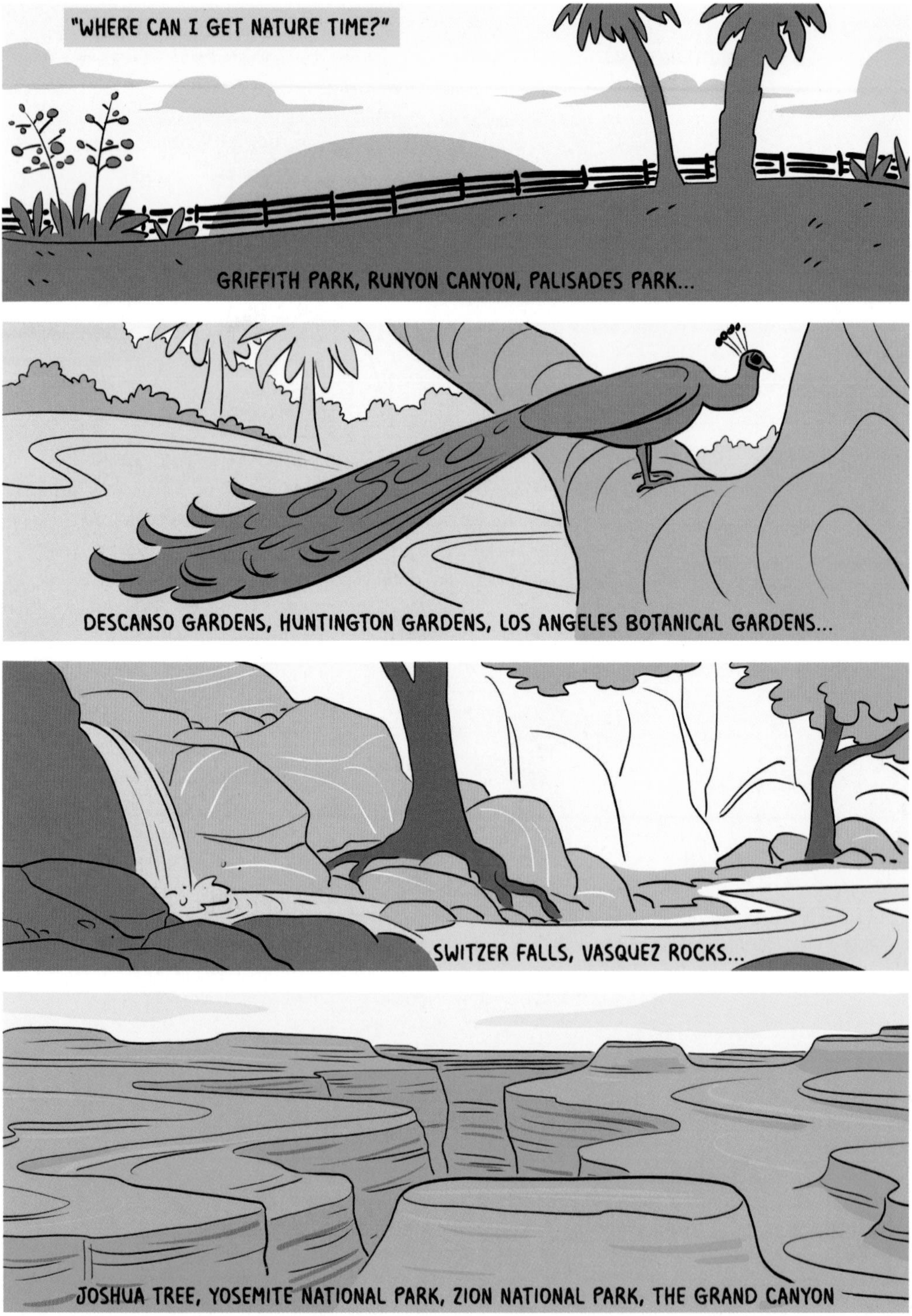
"WHERE CAN I GET NATURE TIME?"
GRIFFITH PARK, RUNYON CANYON, PALISADES PARK...
DESCANSO GARDENS, HUNTINGTON GARDENS, LOS ANGELES BOTANICAL GARDENS...
SWITZER FALLS, VASQUEZ ROCKS...
JOSHUA TREE, YOSEMITE NATIONAL PARK, ZION NATIONAL PARK, THE GRAND CANYON

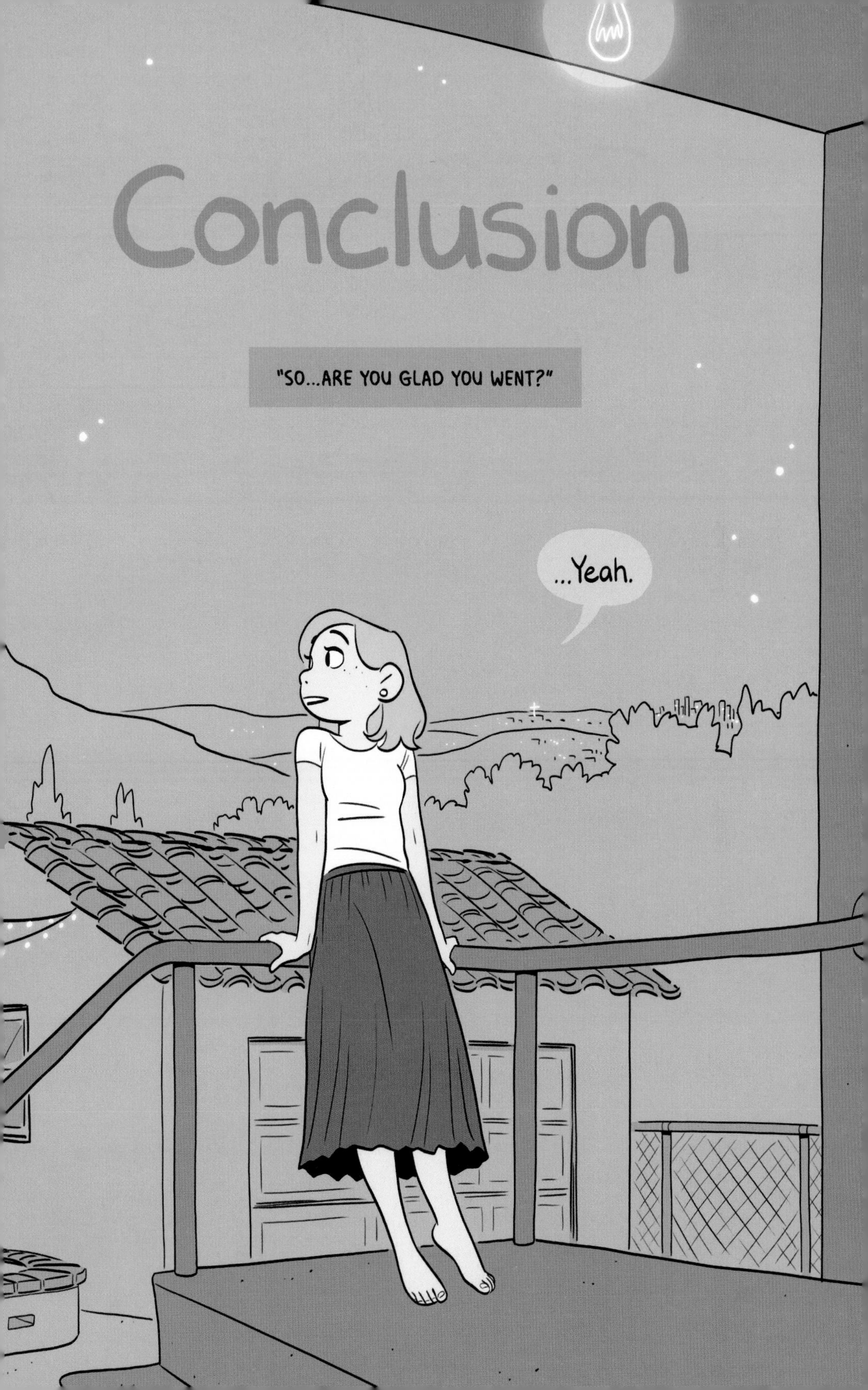
Conclusion
"SO...ARE YOU GLAD YOU WENT?"
...Yeah.

Conclusion

I think it was the right choice for me.

My job is fantastic. I'm learning a lot, giving my resume a serious boost, and I'm still able to work on my own projets on the side!

I'M PUTTING AWAY A LOT OF MONEY FOR MY FUTURE AND I LOVE HAVING GOOD EMPLOYER-SPONSORED HEALTH INSURANCE.

It's gonna be O.K....

RAINY DAY FUNDS

MY FAMILY DOESN'T WORRY ABOUT ME THE WAY THEY DID WHEN I WAS A FREELANCE COMICS CREATOR, AND EVERYONE'S EYES GO WIDE WHEN THEY HEAR THAT I WORK FOR BRANDS THEY RECOGNIZE.

Oh, she finally got a real job??

NOD

There are so many interesting people to meet in L.A., especially artists.

...And I really love the L.A. weather!

But honestly...the first year was hard. Moving somewhere new usually is, but L.A. is just so **BIG**, it was hard to understand the city and find my place here. I got depressed. I saw a therapist for the first time.

And I still miss my family and Portland friends like crazy.

I'VE HEARD L.A. VETERANS SAY :

The first year sucks, but it's not representative of how your life will be here if you stay.

AND IT HAS GOTTEN BETTER THE LONGER I'M HERE, BUT...

Conclusion

...IN THE FUTURE, IF I HAVE THE CHOICE...THERE ARE OTHER CITIES OUT THERE WHERE I COULD LIVE WITHOUT A CAR, CHOOSE SMALL BUSINESSES AND LOCAL ALTERNATIVES TO BIG BOX STORES, USE PUBLIC TRANSPORTATION, MINGLE WITH LOTS OF DIFFERENT KINDS OF PEOPLE EVERY DAY, SEE FRIENDS MORE OFTEN...

...CHILL ON THE BANKS OF A CLEAN RIVER, OR HIKE IN A QUIET FOREST ONCE IN A WHILE.

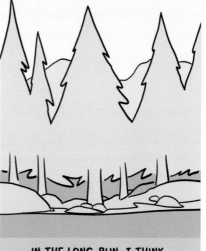

IN THE LONG RUN, I THINK THAT'S WHAT I WANT.

I GOT THROUGH THE LOW POINTS OF MY FIRST YEAR BY TRYING TO DO ONE NEW THING EVERY WEEKEND, TO DISCOVER THE CITY LITTLE BY LITTLE. I TOLD MYSELF,

Learn as much as you can about L.A. while you are here, and that will help you appreciate it.

BECAUSE WHAT IF SOMEDAY I'M BACK IN RAINY HIPSTER PORTLAND, MISSING THE SUNSHINE AND THE DESERT AND MY L.A. FRIENDS?? I WANT TO THINK...

I'm glad I made the most of that time in my life, soaked up every last second, and didn't take it for granted!

IN THAT SPIRIT, I'LL END THIS COMIC WITH A LIST OF GOOD
MEMORIES OF THINGS I'VE DONE & VISITED HERE SO FAR...

PASADENA ROSE BOWL MARKET

MALIBU HIKE, SEEING A BABY SEAL

UCB IMPROV SHOWS

"AT HOME WITH MONSTERS" AT LACMA

SUNSET AT THE GETTY CENTER

MELROSE AVENUE SHOPPING

PASADENA CITY HALL (USED FOR THE EXTERIORS OF PAWNEE CITY HALL IN PARKS & REC)

LA BREA TAR PITS

PICTURE THIS!

Conclusion

VENICE SKATE PARKS

SMORGASBURG

RICHARD III IN GRIFFITH PARK

THE THRILLING ADVENTURE HOUR AT LARGO

TRAIN TO SAN DIEGO

THE OBSERVATORY AT NIGHT

BABY TURTLES IN ECHO PARK

WALKING UNDER SANTA MONICA PIER WITH MY S.O.

BUFFY'S HOUSE & SUNNYDALE HIGH

Conclusion

HOLLYWOOD ESTATE SALES

This guy won Oscars in the 70's for makeup!

Cool...

626 NIGHT MARKET

Takoyaki... in a TACO.

まいう～！！

LADIES AND GENTS NIGHT OUT ON MAGNOLIA BLVD

Free Tarot reading?

Sure!

MAGIC CASTLE

ROOFTOP DRINKS AT PERCH

LAST BOOKSTORE

MORNING ROCK CLIMBING THEN A PINT IN DTLA

END-OF-THE-NIGHT DINNER FROM TACO TRUCKS

RUPAUL'S DRAGCON

Conclusion

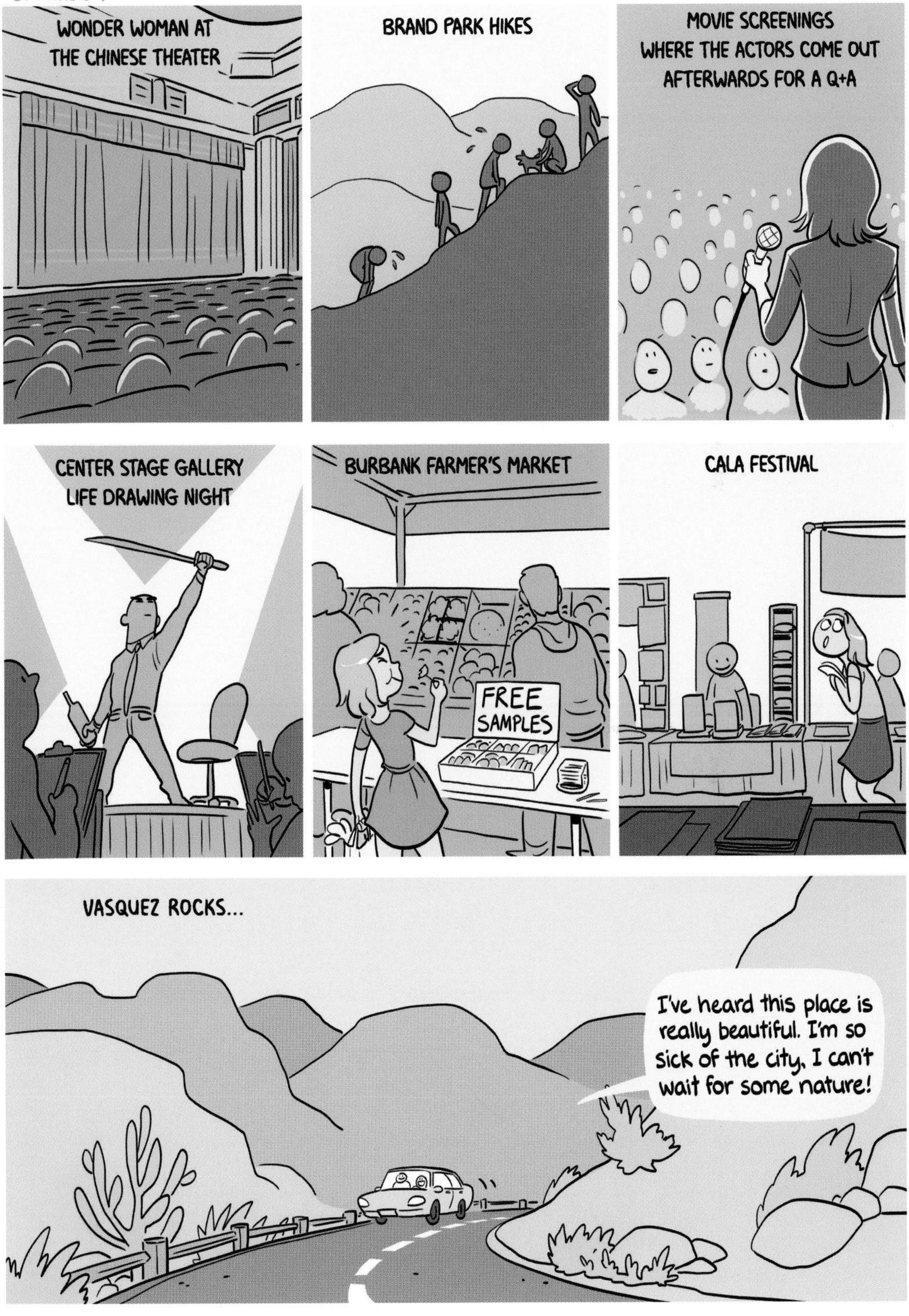
WONDER WOMAN AT THE CHINESE THEATER
BRAND PARK HIKES
MOVIE SCREENINGS WHERE THE ACTORS COME OUT AFTERWARDS FOR A Q+A
CENTER STAGE GALLERY LIFE DRAWING NIGHT
BURBANK FARMER'S MARKET
FREE SAMPLES
CALA FESTIVAL
VASQUEZ ROCKS...
I've heard this place is really beautiful. I'm so sick of the city, I can't wait for some nature!

Conclusion

...

It's just...BROWN.

THIS is where people told me to go when I said I missed nature. THIS is the best L.A. has got???

It's ugly as hell!

1 HOUR LATER :

Huh, the mountains in the distance are kind of pretty. They almost look blue compared to all of the brown.

1 HOUR LATER :

I think...maybe my eyes are adjusting? I'm seeing a lot of different colors now.

END OF THE DAY :

It's....BEAUTIFUL!

MAYBE L.A. IS JUST AN ACQUIRED TASTE LIKE THAT...MAYBE IT TAKES SOME TIME FOR YOUR EYES TO ADJUST.

Alternate P.O.V.s

NOW THAT YOU'VE READ ALL ABOUT HOW I FEEL, WHY DON'T WE GET SOME **OTHER** ANIMATION PROS IN HERE TO SHARE THEIR POINTS OF VIEW?

P.O.V.: Angie Wang

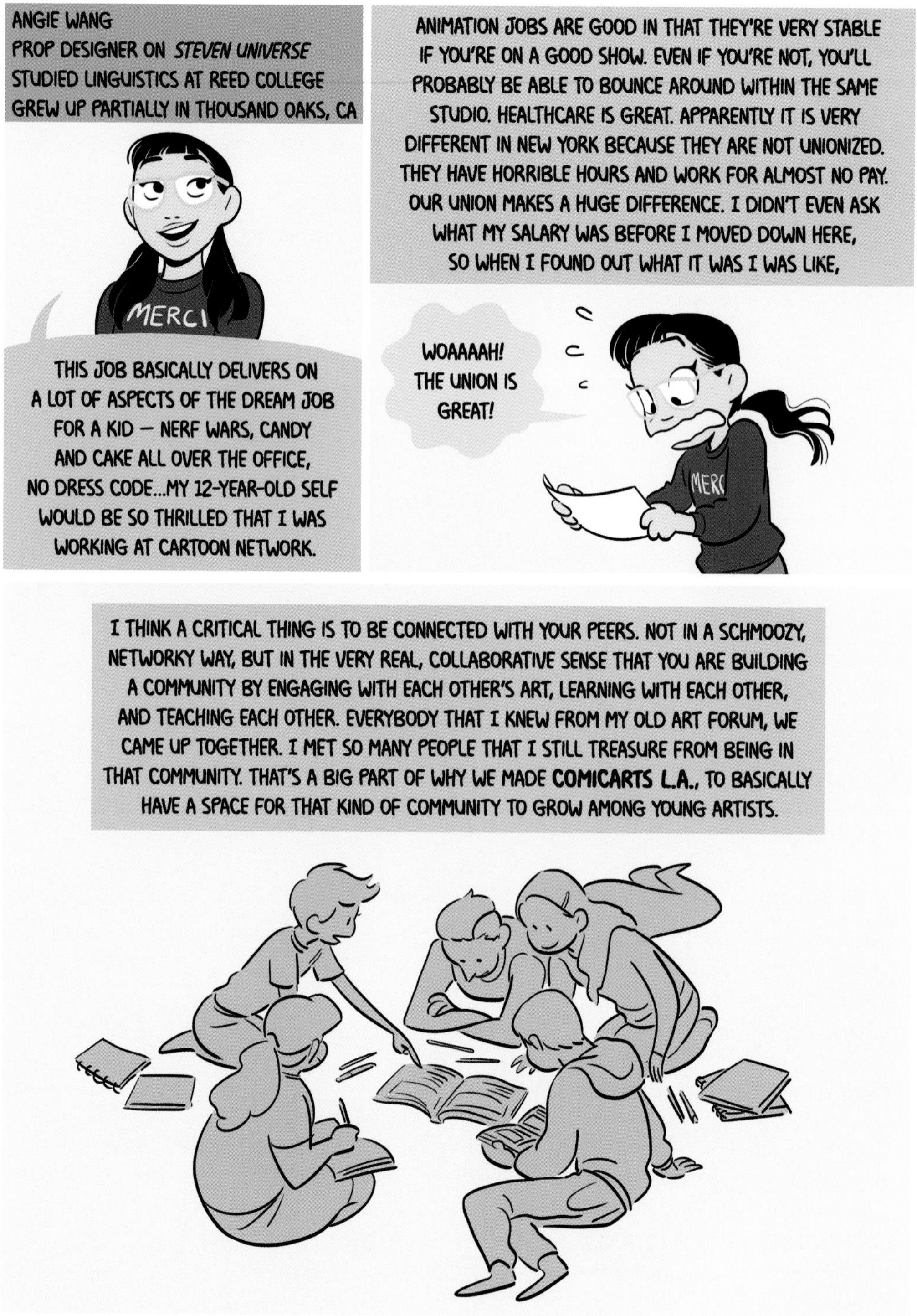
ANGIE WANG
PROP DESIGNER ON STEVEN UNIVERSE
STUDIED LINGUISTICS AT REED COLLEGE
GREW UP PARTIALLY IN THOUSAND OAKS, CA
MERCI
THIS JOB BASICALLY DELIVERS ON A LOT OF ASPECTS OF THE DREAM JOB FOR A KID — NERF WARS, CANDY AND CAKE ALL OVER THE OFFICE, NO DRESS CODE...MY 12-YEAR-OLD SELF WOULD BE SO THRILLED THAT I WAS WORKING AT CARTOON NETWORK.
ANIMATION JOBS ARE GOOD IN THAT THEY'RE VERY STABLE IF YOU'RE ON A GOOD SHOW. EVEN IF YOU'RE NOT, YOU'LL PROBABLY BE ABLE TO BOUNCE AROUND WITHIN THE SAME STUDIO. HEALTHCARE IS GREAT. APPARENTLY IT IS VERY DIFFERENT IN NEW YORK BECAUSE THEY ARE NOT UNIONIZED. THEY HAVE HORRIBLE HOURS AND WORK FOR ALMOST NO PAY. OUR UNION MAKES A HUGE DIFFERENCE. I DIDN'T EVEN ASK WHAT MY SALARY WAS BEFORE I MOVED DOWN HERE, SO WHEN I FOUND OUT WHAT IT WAS I WAS LIKE,
WOAAAAH! THE UNION IS GREAT!
I THINK A CRITICAL THING IS TO BE CONNECTED WITH YOUR PEERS. NOT IN A SCHMOOZY, NETWORKY WAY, BUT IN THE VERY REAL, COLLABORATIVE SENSE THAT YOU ARE BUILDING A COMMUNITY BY ENGAGING WITH EACH OTHER'S ART, LEARNING WITH EACH OTHER, AND TEACHING EACH OTHER. EVERYBODY THAT I KNEW FROM MY OLD ART FORUM, WE CAME UP TOGETHER. I MET SO MANY PEOPLE THAT I STILL TREASURE FROM BEING IN THAT COMMUNITY. THAT'S A BIG PART OF WHY WE MADE COMICARTS L.A., TO BASICALLY HAVE A SPACE FOR THAT KIND OF COMMUNITY TO GROW AMONG YOUNG ARTISTS.

WORKING IN ANIMATION HAS BEEN A VERY POSITIVE EXPERIENCE FOR ME. THIS IS GOING TO SOUND TERRIBLE, BUT A BIG THING I LOVE ABOUT MY JOB IS JUST THAT IT'S A VERY MINDLESS DRAWING EXPERIENCE.

FOR A VERY LONG TIME MY WORK, MY HOBBY, AND MY FREETIME WAS ALL DRAWING. WORKING IN ANIMATION HAS ALLOWED ME TO DEVELOP ACTUAL HOBBIES, SUCH AS FITNESS! AND POLE DANCE! AND AERIALS! IT'S VERY NEW TO ME.

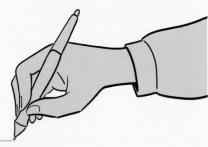

WHEN I DOODLE, WHAT I REALLY WANT TO DO IS MINDLESSLY DRAW SOMETHING THAT LOOKS NICE AND JUST TURN MY BRAIN OFF AND NOODLE AROUND. I FEEL LIKE ANIMATION IS A GOOD PLACE TO DO THAT AND GET PAID. FOR OTHER PEOPLE IT'S A MUCH MORE ROMANTIC THING, BUT FOR ME, I LIKE THAT IT'S TECHNICAL, IT'S MEDITATIVE, AND I GET SAVE MY CONCEPTUAL BRAIN POWER FOR MY ILLUSTRATIONS OR FOR MY OWN PROJECTS INSTEAD.

I THINK THE INTEREST IN FITNESS AND ALSO THE LEISURE TIME TO HAVE A WORK / LIFE BALANCE IS VERY L.A. I KNOW IT'S NOT THE SAME IN NEW YORK, WHERE PEOPLE ARE MUCH MORE LIKE, "IF YOU'RE NOT WORKING, YOU'RE NETWORKING." YOU'RE HAVING LUNCH WITH THE ART DIRECTORS OR A BUNCH OF OTHER ILLUSTRATORS. L.A. IS MORE LIKE, YOU'RE ALLOWED TO HAVE AN ACTUAL **LIFE**. EVERYBODY I KNOW IN L.A. WHO IS AN ANIMATOR OR ILLUSTRATOR HAS A HOBBY BEYOND DRAWING. PLUS IT'S SUCH A BIG CITY, YOU CAN FIND A CLASS AND PEERS FOR WHATEVER YOU'RE INTO. I LOVE THAT I'M TOTALLY SPOILED FOR CHOICE IN TERMS OF WHAT POLE STUDIOS I CAN GO TO. THERE ARE LIKE FIVE WITHIN FIVE MILES OF ME.

I LOVE IT HERE. EVEN THE TRAFFIC'S NOT TOO BAD CUZ YOU GET TO HANG OUT AND LISTEN TO PODCASTS. THE HEAT IS THE ONLY BAD THING. I LOVE IT HERE. I'M REALLY SURPRISED TO SAY THAT...CUZ I ALWAYS THOUGHT I'D HATE L.A. AND THERE IS SOMETHING ABOUT L.A. WHERE IT'S LIKE, **SO UGLY** THAT WHEN YOU LOVE IT, YOU FEEL REALLY SPECIAL FOR LOVING IT. I LOVE THE SENSE THAT EVERYBODY HERE IS TRYING TO MAKE IT.

ANTOINE ETTORI
STORY ARTIST ON *SING 2*
GREW UP IN SW FRANCE
STUDIED ART AT EMILE COHL

I FIRST STUDIED ENGINEERING. AFTER I GRADUATED, I DECIDED TO GIVE ART A TRY.

I THINK IT'S SOMETHING I HAVE IN ME SINCE MY CHILDHOOD. MY PARENTS LOVE CINEMA, DRAWING, COMIC BOOKS AND ART IN GENERAL. IT LEAD ME TO DRAW A LOT AND TELL STORIES SINCE MY CHILDHOOD. AT FIRST I ONLY DREW FOR MYSELF, BUT AT A POINT I JUST DECIDED TO TRY TO MAKE A LIVING OF MY DRAWINGS. AND SO FAR IT WORKS. I'VE NEVER REALLY BEEN STRESSED BY FINDING A JOB BECAUSE I COME FROM A VERY DIFFERENT ENVIRONMENT AND JUST DRAWING FOR MYSELF WOULD BE NICE, TOO. EVERY SINGLE DRAWING I'M PAID FOR IS A BONUS!

MY FIRST JOB WAS DURING OUR INTERNSHIP PROGRAM AT SCHOOL. I WORKED ON A DOCUMENTARY MIXING LIVE FOOTAGE AND 2D TRADITIONAL ANIMATION. IT WAS DIFFICULT BUT INTERESTING AND FOR THE FIRST TIME MY WORK WAS BROADCAST ON TV.

I MOVED A LOT BEFORE FINALLY SETTLING IN PARIS WHEN I FOUND A JOB AS A STORY ARTIST ON A TV SHOW NAMED *KAELOO*.

I'VE ALWAYS WANTED TO TELL STORIES. BUT WORKING IN ANIMATION IS MORE OF A PRAGMATIC CHOICE. I LOVE MY JOB, BUT WHAT I LOVE DEEP INSIDE IS **DRAWING**. I CHOSE STORYBOARDING BECAUSE IT GATHERS MULTIPLE ASPECTS OF DRAWING THAT I LOVE. LIKE ANIMATION, DRAWING BACKGROUNDS, CHARACTER DESIGN, STORYTELLING, ETC...

I'M REALLY GLAD I PURSUED ANIMATION. HONESTLY I DON'T REALLY SEE ANY NEGATIVE ASPECT TO MY WORK. IT CAN BE STRESSFUL SOMETIMES OR BORING BECAUSE OF THE PRODUCTION PROCESS, BUT IT'S MOSTLY NICE TO WORK IN THE ANIMATION INDUSTRY. AND I WOULD OF COURSE ENCOURAGE ANYONE TO GIVE IT A TRY.

THE SWITCH BETWEEN DRAWING FOR YOURSELF AND FOR A STUDIO CAN BE A BIG THING, BUT YOU'LL LEARN A LOT ABOUT YOUR ART DOING THAT. AND YOU'LL GET BETTER AT WORK. IT'S A POSITIVE CIRCLE.

I FELT VERY LUCKY TO BE RECRUITED BY AN AMERICAN STUDIO IN 2016. IT WAS REALLY EXCITING ; LIKE A BIG PAID VACATION IN A WAY. GETTING THE VISAS WAS A BIT STRESSFUL BECAUSE OF ALL THE BACK AND FORTH WITH IMMIGRATION. BUT MOVING WAS A BONUS, AN INTERESTING EXPERIENCE AND SOMETHING I'D NEVER DREAMED OF.

HAVING WORKED IN BOTH, I'D SAY THE MAIN DIFFERENCE BETWEEN PRODUCTIONS IN FRANCE AND THE U.S. IS THE BUDGET YOU HAVE TO PRODUCE MOVIES. THIS GENERATES DIFFERENCES AT A DAILY WORK LEVEL. FOR EXAMPLE IN FRANCE FOR FINANCIAL REASONS YOU DON'T SPEND TOO MUCH TIME REWRITING SCRIPTS – MOST OF THE TIME YOUR FIRST DRAFT IS YOUR FINAL DRAFT. SINCE YOU HAVE LESS MONEY, YOU HAVE LESS PEOPLE WORKING ON A SHOW, CONSEQUENTLY PEOPLE IN FRANCE ARE USUALLY ABLE TO DO MULTIPLE TASKS.

I LATER LEFT L.A. BECAUSE I DIVORCED AND MY EX-WIFE WANTED TO COME BACK TO FRANCE WITH OUR KIDS. STAYING IN THE U.S. WASN'T REALLY AN OPTION FROM THE BEGINNING. I LOVE EUROPE TOO MUCH, AND PARIS AND MY FAMILY.

THE BEST PART ABOUT WORKING IN ANIMATION IS MEETING PEOPLE FROM EVERYWHERE AND CREATING A STORY THAT WILL IMPACT PEOPLE.

KEEP DRAWING, AND ALWAYS KEEP LEARNING. NOT ONLY ANIMATION. BUT WATCH MOVIES, READ BOOKS, GO TO MUSEUMS, ETC... I THINK THE MORE YOU DISCOVER THE WORLD, THE BETTER YOU'LL BE AT TELLING STORIES. SOMETIMES I FEEL PEOPLE DRAW THINGS IN A CERTAIN WAY BECAUSE IT'S TRENDING, BUT WITHOUT UNDERSTANDING HOW PEOPLE GOT TO DRAW LIKE THAT. THERE'S NOTHING LIKE UNDERSTANDING THE NARRATIVE PROCESS OF GREAT DIRECTORS WHEN YOU STORYBOARD.

DAVE PIMENTEL, CO-DIRECTOR ON *DARKMOUTH* AT ALCON ENTERTAINMENT GREW UP IN LOS SERRANOS, CALIFORNIA STUDIED ANIMATION AT CAL-ARTS

I LEFT MY PARENTS' HOME FOR CALARTS WHEN I WAS 22. FIRST TIME OUT OF THE HOUSE. VERY NAIVE AND VERY SCARED.

I WAS ALWAYS AN ARTIST AT HEART, ALWAYS DRAWING. I WAS IN A JUNIOR COLLEGE TAKING EVERY ART CLASS I COULD, JUST TO KEEP FULFILLING THAT NEED OF CREATION. I DIDN'T KNOW WHERE IT WAS GOING TO GO —I WAS AIRBRUSHING, DRAWING AS MUCH AS I COULD ... AND I WENT TO AN "ANIMATION ART" SHOW AT A GALLERY. I SAW ROUGH DRAWINGS UP ON THE WALL. THE LIGHT BULB WENT OFF AND THE ANGELS SANG.

THAT'S IT. THAT'S WHAT I WANT TO DO.

FROM THERE FORWARD I STARTED TO SEARCH : WHERE CAN I LEARN IT, WHAT CAN I DO, WHERE CAN I GO. THAT WAS IN 1989. I FIGURED OUT THAT CALARTS WAS THE PLACE I WANTED TO GO, AND GOT THERE IN '92, AND THEN GOT OUT OF THERE IN '94, BECAUSE I COULDN'T AFFORD IT.

I GOT AN INTERNSHIP. THE PROGRAM WAS A LITTLE BIT OF EVERYTHING, SO I DID FX, ANIMATION, AND STORYBOARDING. THEY JUST WANTED TO SEE WHERE I WOULD BLOSSOM. I OBVIOUSLY WANTED TO BE A HAND-DRAWN (2-D) ANIMATOR, BECAUSE THAT WAS MY MAIN FOCUS AT SCHOOL. I GOT A "CLEAN-UP" JOB IN A FEATURE STUDIO, STARTED DOING IN-BETWEEN CLEAN-UP. I WORKED MY WAY FROM THERE UP TO BEING AN ANIMATOR

WHEN I SAW THE REELS FOR *TOY STORY*, I KNEW THAT CG WAS COMING. I KNEW THAT 2-D'S DAYS WERE NUMBERED. SO I STARTED TO DO STORYBOARD TESTS AND CG ANIMATION TESTS. I WAS DOING THE BOUNCING BALL AND THE GUY CARRYING THE HEAVY BAG OR HEAVY ROCK AND PUSHING IT OVER A WALL. EARLY IN MY CAREER, YOU COULD DO A TEST LIKE THAT AND IF YOU KNEW YOUR WAY AROUND IT, THEY WOULD TRAIN YOU. NOWADAYS YOU HAVE TO SHOW PERFORMANCE AND FULL-ON ACTING AND ALL THAT. I WOULD STAY LATE, COME IN ON WEEKENDS, AND DO STORYBOARD TESTS. I HAD STORYBOARDED TWO SHORTS, THEY WEREN'T GREAT, BUT THEY HAD A BEGINNING, MIDDLE, AND END. I SUBMITTED BOTH. MY HEART WAS IN THE STORY PART, BECAUSE I WOULD CONTINUE TO DRAW.

THE NEXT DAY, AN EXECUTIVE AND A DIRECTOR BURST OPEN THE DOOR AND SAID, "DO YOU WANT TO BE IN STORY?" I DROPPED THE ANIMATION SCENE I WAS ON,

TO HELL WITH THIS! I'M IN **STORY**! WHOO HOO!

A LOT OF TIMES, BACK IN THE DAY AND NOW, ARTISTS COME UP TO PROFESSIONALS AND SAY,

I CAN DO IT **ALL**.

IT DOESN'T WORK THAT WAY IN THIS BUSINESS. MAYBE YOU COULD, BUT I NEED TO BE ABLE TO PLUG YOU INTO MY MACHINE AND HAVE YOU PRODUCE WHAT I NEED YOU TO DO. IT'S BETTER TO HAVE A SPECIALTY.

FOCUS YOUR PORTFOLIO ON YOUR **TOP** STRENGTH — ONCE YOU GET INTO A JOB FOR THAT, AND YOU GET THROUGH A MOVIE DOING THAT ONE JOB, THEN WHEN YOU'RE IN AND YOU'RE SAFE AND GOOD, YOU CAN START TO EXPLORE THOSE OTHER INTERESTS.

ANIMATOR

FX ARTIST

STORY ARTIST

CHARACTER DESIGNER

WRITER

WOULD YOU RECOMMEND ANIMATION AS A CAREER PATH?

100%. BUT IT TAKES MANY HOURS. YOUR SKILL LEVEL IS GOING TO CORRELATE TO THE STUDIO YOU WORK FOR. YOU WANT TO WORK FOR A TOP STUDIO? YOU GOTTA BE AT THAT LEVEL. IF YOU DON'T PUT IN THE TIME AND ENERGY TO GET TO THAT LEVEL, THEN YOU'RE NOT GONNA WORK AT THAT STUDIO. YOU MIGHT HAVE TO WORK AT A LESSER STUDIO AND LET THAT TOP STUDIO BE A DESTINATION THAT YOU CAN EVOLVE TO.

THE HARDEST TRANSITION FOR ME WAS JUST BEING ALONE. COMING TO AN UNKNOWN PLACE AND BEING A-**LONE**. I DIDN'T KNOW ANYBODY. THAT WAS MY FIRST TIME MOVING OUT. I THOUGHT I WAS GOING TO GET HURT OR BEAT UP, OR SOMETHING WAS GOING TO HAPPEN TO ME, CUZ I WAS THE BABY OF THE FAMILY! 8 BROTHERS AND SISTERS. ALSO I WAS KIND OF SHELTERED BECAUSE, PHYSICALLY, MY EYES AREN'T LIKE OTHERS, THEY'RE A LITTLE OFF IN POSITION. THAT'S HOW I WAS BORN. AS A KID, YOU'RE OVER-PROTECTED, AND I HAD TO BREAK THROUGH THAT.

I'M AN INDIVIDUAL! I'M INDEPENDENT!

LEAVING HOME

I'M SO SCARED...!!

FIRST DAY IN THE DORMS

BUT I MADE FRIENDS QUICKLY. AND THE BEST THING ABOUT COMING HERE WAS FINDING MY PEOPLE.

CALARTS WAS FULL OF LIKE-MINDED PEOPLE WHO COULD SPEAK ON GEEK-TERMS LIKE YOU, THAT WAS SO AMAZING. EVERYBODY WAS SO COOL. THEY WERE ALL THE MISFITS WHO CAME FROM THEIR PARTICULAR CITY TO CONGLOMERATE INTO THIS ONE GROUP OF PEOPLE AND UNITE. I FIND, MOST OF THE TIME, 90% OF THE ARTISTS THAT I'VE EVER MET OR COME ACROSS HAVE ALL BEEN SUPER COOL. THEY WENT THROUGH SIMILAR ISSUES THAT I DID.

THE BEST THING IS, YOU'RE CREATING A PIECE OF ARTWORK THAT GENERATES A REACTION. YOU HAVE A PIECE OF PAPER, YOU DO A DRAWING ON IT, AND SOMEONE GOES, "HA!" AND THEY SMILE. OR THEY GO, "WHAT HAPPENED? WHY IS THIS CHARACTER SAD?" THAT REACTION IS THE GREATEST THING IN THE WORLD TO ME. IT COMES FROM WHEN YOU'RE A KID AND YOU GO TO YOUR MOM AND SAY, "LOOK WHAT I DID!" AND THEY'RE LIKE, "AW, BEAUTIFUL," AND THEY PUT IT ON THE FRIDGE.

THE WORST THING IS WHEN YOU'RE SENT OFF ON A PATH YOU KNOW IS NOT GOOD, AND YOU STILL HAVE TO DO IT, CUZ THAT'S YOUR JOB. YOU HAVE TO DROP YOUR EXPECTATION FROM, "I'M SUPER CREATIVE!" TO, "I NEED TO KEEP MY JOB AND SEE IF I CAN SOLVE THIS." THAT MOMENT WHERE YOU'RE LIKE, "I DON'T BELIEVE IN THIS AND I STILL HAVE TO DO IT," IS PROBABLY THE WORST THING. SOMETIMES YOU FIND A GEM IN THE PROCESS OF DRUDGING THROUGH THE SEQUENCE, THEN YOU'RE ULTIMATELY BACK TO BEING SUPER CREATIVE! BUT SOMETIMES NOT, HAHA! BUT IT'S POSSIBLE AND THAT'S THE END GOAL ANYWAYS.

ONLY THE INSECURE ARTISTS ARE COMPETITIVE. IF SOMEONE HASN'T WORKED HARD ENOUGH, THEY MAY SEE ANOTHER ARTIST AS A THREAT. THEY WON'T EVER ADMIT THAT THEY HAVEN'T DONE ENOUGH WORK, BUT I THINK IF THERE'S THAT KIND OF NOT-NICENESS, IT'S BECAUSE THEY PROBABLY HAVEN'T DONE ENOUGH FOR THEMSELVES AND THEY'RE WORRIED YOU'RE GONNA COME IN AND TAKE THEIR SPOT.

I'VE TAUGHT ARTISTS, AND I'LL TELL YOU EVERYTHING YOU NEED TO KNOW, BECAUSE THAT'S YOUR PATH. YOU STILL HAVE TO DO THE WORK. I'LL TELL YOU EVERYTHING. GO AHEAD. CUZ I'M OVER HERE, I'M ON MY PATH. IF I KEEP WORKING HARD AT IT, I'LL BE OK.

STUDY STORY THEORY AS EARLY AS POSSIBLE. IT TOOK ME A LONG TIME TO GET TO HERE. IT'S NOT EASY, BECAUSE EVERY STORY IS NEW, NO MATTER HOW MUCH YOU KNOW. YOU HAVE TO FIND THE NEW TWISTS AND TURNS OF THAT STORY.

I LIKE TELLING STORIES, SO IT WAS PERFECT FOR ME TO GO THROUGH STORY. I LOVE... EVEN DOING THIS! I'M EMOTING A STORY FOR YOU. WHERE I'M AT IS PERFECT FOR ME. FOR NOW.

SET YOUR GOAL AS HIGH AS YOU CAN. IF YOU WANT TO BE A DIRECTOR, WHAT IS THE PATH TO GET THERE? MAYBE THE PATH GOES THROUGH ANIMATION AND STORY...BUT KNOWING MY GOAL WOULD PROBABLY HAVE ALLOWED ME TO STUDY MORE CLEARLY IN A DIRECTION.

DIANA HUH
BOARD ARTIST ON *SHE-RA*
FROM PORTLAND, OREGON
STUDIED HISTORY, FILM AT UCLA

I THINK A LOT OF BREAKING IN IS, UNFORTUNATELY, LUCK AND TIMING.

IT'S REALLY IMPORTANT TO BE HERE IN L.A., BUT BECAUSE L.A. IS SO EXPENSIVE, I WOULDN'T ENCOURAGE PEOPLE TO MOVE HERE JUST ON THE **PROSPECT** OF A JOB. I RECOMMEND PEOPLE DO BOARDS OF THEIR OWN, PUT THEM ONLINE, AND LOOK FOR OPPORTUNITIES. IT'S A SLOW PROCESS, SO TRY NOT TO GET JEALOUS IF IT'S FASTER FOR OTHERS. EVERYBODY'S JOURNEY IS DIFFERENT.

I WOULD RECOMMEND BEING ACTIVE ON SOCIAL MEDIA, PROBABLY THE BEST AND CHEAPEST WAY TO DO IT.

IT'S ALSO IMPORTANT TO BE A NICE, DECENT PERSON. IT'S OK TO BE A LITTLE GREEN AT FIRST. AS LONG AS YOU'RE DECENT, PEOPLE WILL GIVE YOU CHANCES.

LOTS OF BOARD ARTISTS POST THEIR SEQUENCES ON TWITTER. STUDY THEIR BOARDS AND LEARN FROM THEM – I STILL DO THAT TO THIS DAY!

ALL OF MY JOBS WERE BECAUSE OF RECOMMENDATIONS BY FRIENDS. IF YOU'RE NOT A NICE PERSON, AND YOU'RE ALSO NOT GOOD AT YOUR JOB, **NO ONE'S** GONNA WANT TO HIRE YOU.

AND JUST BOARD YOUR OWN STUFF! SURPRISINGLY, A LOT OF ASPIRING BOARD ARTISTS DO NOT HAVE BOARDS OF THEIR OWN. IF ALL YOU HAVE IS NICE ILLUSTRATIONS IN YOUR PORTFOLIO, HOW IS ANYBODY SUPPOSED TO TRUST THAT YOU CAN DO ANYTHING BUT ILLUSTRATION?

I WANT TO BE A STORYBOARD ARTIST!

COOL! BUT... WHERE ARE YOUR **BOARDS?**

WHILE MY FILM SCHOOL EXPERIENCE PREPARED ME FOR THE BASICS OF FILMMAKING, I HAVE NEVER BEEN PREPARED FOR ANY OF THE PRODUCTIONS I'VE BEEN ON. THERE'S A LEARNING CURVE EVERY TIME, AND THAT'S OKAY.

THE GREAT THING ABOUT ANIMATION IS THAT YOU LEARN ON THE JOB. I HAD NO ACTION BOARD EXPERIENCE BEFORE MY CURRENT SHOW. BUT BECAUSE MY DIRECTORS WERE WILLING TO TEACH ME, AND I WANTED TO LEARN, I BECAME A MUCH STRONGER BOARD ARTIST.

I KNOW A FEW ARTISTS WHO AREN'T VERY GRACIOUS WITH THEIR DIRECTORS AND I'M LIKE, "YOU'RE NOT GONNA MAKE IT." THIS IS THEIR FIRST SHOW, THERE'S NO WAY ANYONE WILL WANT TO WORK WITH THAT RIGIDITY, ESPECIALLY IF THEY'RE INEXPERIENCED AND YOUNG.

IT'S OK TO MAKE MISTAKES AS LONG AS YOU'RE WILLING TO **LEARN**, THAT'S ALL IT IS.

I DO TRULY BELIEVE THAT ANIMATION IS A HELPFUL COMMUNITY AND WE WANT TO SEE EACH OTHER FLOURISH. BUT I WISH THAT THE STUDIO PIPELINE FACILITATED MENTORSHIP BETWEEN NEW ARTISTS AND ESTABLISHED ARTISTS....

ANIMATION IS A TOUGH INDUSTRY TO NAVIGATE ON YOUR OWN, AND YOU CAN'T EXPECT TO HAVE YOUR HAND HELD THE WHOLE TIME, ESPECIALLY IN TV. THAT'S WHY I WANT THOSE OF US ALREADY IN THE INDUSTRY TO HELP GUIDE THE NEW ARTISTS COMING IN.

I WAS LUCKY THAT I COULD FIND SUPPORT AND GUIDANCE IN MY EARLY YEARS, BUT I'VE STILL HAD ROUGH PATCHES IN ANIMATION. I DON'T REGRET ANY OF IT THOUGH. I KNOW NOW TO TRUST MY TASTE, TRUST MY VALUE. IF YOU HAVE ANYTHING WORTH SAYING, YOU GOTTA PROTECT IT. DON'T CHANGE THE STORIES YOU WANT TO TELL JUST BECAUSE OF EVERYBODY ELSE. DON'T LET PEOPLE THINK YOU'RE LESS VALUABLE THAN YOU REALLY ARE.

P.O.V.: Diana Huh

SO DON'T BE AFRAID TO PUT YOURSELF OUT THERE! SOMETIMES PEOPLE WILL DISAGREE WITH YOUR IDEAS, BUT KNOW THAT BEING WRONG IS NOT A WEAKNESS. IT'S NOT A LOSING SCENARIO. SOMETIMES YOUR WHOLE BOARD WILL GET SCRAPPED, AND IT'LL HURT, BUT THAT'S OKAY. ANIMATION IS COLLABORATION, AND LEARNING HOW TO COMBINE YOUR IDEAS WITH YOUR FELLOW ARTISTS WILL MAKE YOU A STRONGER STORYTELLER.

TAKE CARE OF YOURSELF ONCE YOU'RE IN THE INDUSTRY, BUT ONCE YOU HAVE A FEW YEARS UNDER YOUR BELT, PLEASE TRY TAKE CARE OF THE PEOPLE AROUND YOU, TOO. OUR INDUSTRY CAN ONLY FLOURISH IF WE SUPPORT AND HELP EACH OTHER.

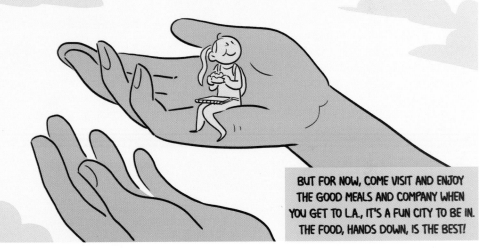

BUT FOR NOW, COME VISIT AND ENJOY THE GOOD MEALS AND COMPANY WHEN YOU GET TO L.A., IT'S A FUN CITY TO BE IN. THE FOOD, HANDS DOWN, IS THE BEST!

AND ON A PERSONAL LEVEL, BEING IN L.A. LET ME HAVE MORE PRIDE IN MY BACKGROUND. I DIDN'T REALIZE HOW MUCH OF THE MICRO-AGGRESSIONS I GREW UP WITH FORMED MY PERSONALITY AND HOW I REACTED TO THINGS UNTIL I MOVED HERE. L.A. IS A WONDERFUL CITY THAT MADE ME FEEL PROUD TO BE KOREAN AMERICAN, AND I TRY TO REFLECT THAT PRIDE IN HOW I LIVE AND WORK EVERY DAY.

DREW GREEN
STORY ARTIST ON *CRAIG OF THE CREEK*
FROM ATLANTA, GEORGIA

I'M A HIGH SCHOOL GRADUATE. EVERYTHING I NEEDED TO KNOW, I LEARNED FROM THE INTERNET, FROM FRIENDS, AND FROM SIMPLY MAKING THINGS!

I ALWAYS KNEW I WANTED TO BE AN ARTIST OF SOME SORT. AS A KID, I WAS CONSTANTLY DRAWING CARTOON, COMIC, AND VIDEO GAME CHARACTERS, BUT GREW UP NOT REALLY THINKING IT COULD BE A CAREER. IN HIGH SCHOOL, I BRIEFLY CONSIDERED A CAREER IN GRAPHIC DESIGN AS IT WAS THE ONLY CREATIVE JOB I WAS TOLD MIGHT PROVIDE A DECENT LIVING — WHEN YOU'RE IN HIGH SCHOOL, EVERYONE SEEMS SO CONCERNED ABOUT HOW MUCH MONEY YOU'RE GOING TO MAKE AND IT HAS A WAY OF SEEPING INTO YOUR HEAD!

I MADE MY FIRST TRIP TO THE WEST COAST WHEN A FRIEND SUGGESTED I VISIT BURBANK FOR CTNX (CREATIVE TALENT NETWORK EXPO). I WAS TIRED OF JUST GETTING BY IN ATLANTA WITH A LITTLE MONEY FROM DOING COMMISSIONS AND THE ODD FREELANCE GIG. I WAS UNCOMFORTABLE AND EXHAUSTED AND THE AMOUNT OF EFFORT WASN'T PAYING OFF IN A MEANINGFUL WAY.

I PACKED MY CAR AND MOVED ACROSS THE COUNTRY, HAD A LOT OF LUNCHES WITH PEOPLE IN THE INDUSTRY WHO I KNEW VIA THE INTERNET OR MERELY KNEW OF, AND PICKED A LOT OF BRAINS.

ULTIMATELY, IT WAS MY SOCIAL MEDIA CONNECTIONS THAT PAID OFF IN THE FORM OF A JOB.

SO DRAW AND POST OFTEN!

I GOT FEEDBACK ON MY PORTFOLIO FROM A LOT OF WORKING ARTISTS TABLING AT THE CONVENTION. THAT EXPERIENCE REALLY HELPED OPEN MY EYES TO THE IDEA OF MOVING TO CALIFORNIA AND PURSUING A CAREER IN THE INDUSTRY.

P.O.V. : Drew Green

I'M VERY GLAD I PURSUED ANIMATION AS A CAREER. MY DRAWING SKILLS IMPROVED TENFOLD SIMPLY BY DRAWING SO MUCH EVERY DAY. I PRETTY MUCH NEVER COME INTO WORK DREADING THE TASK AT HAND.

IF YOU'RE GOING TO BE LIVING WITH A FRIEND FOR A BIT WHILE YOU GET ON YOUR FEET HERE, MAKE SURE THE TERMS OF THE AGREEMENT ARE REALLY CLEAR. I FOUND MYSELF IN A SITUATION WHERE THE TERMS WERE NOT CLEAR AND I ENDED UP TAKING ADVANTAGE OF SOMEONE'S HOSPITALITY, SOMETHING THAT EXPLODED IN A REALLY UNPLEASANT WAY, AND SOMETHING THAT I DEEPLY REGRET. A ROCKY START TO MY L.A. JOURNEY, FOR SURE.

I FEEL VERY FORTUNATE - IT'S A PRIVILEGE AND I DON'T TAKE IT FOR GRANTED. I WOULD ENCOURAGE A YOUNG PERSON TO PURSUE IT IF THEY KNOW GOING IN THAT IT'S A LOT OF **WORK**, AND THAT DOING A LOT OF WORK ISN'T NECESSARILY A BAD THING.

IT'S A VERY DIVERSE TOWN IN EVERY SENSE OF THE WORD. PARTICULARLY IF YOU END UP IN ANIMATION. YOU'LL DEFINITELY FIND YOUR CROWD AND IT'LL FEEL AT LEAST SOMEWHAT LIKE HOME IN A YEAR OR TWO.

IN REGARDS TO LOOKING FORWARD TO YOUR ANIMATION CAREER : IT'S OKAY TO START SMALL. I REALIZE IT'S FUNNY HEARING THIS FROM SOMEONE WHO WAS LUCKY ENOUGH TO JUMP RIGHT INTO BEING A STORYBOARD ARTIST, BUT THERE'S NOTHING WRONG WITH LEARNING THE ROPES AS A PRODUCTION ASSISTANT OR A STORYBOARD REVISIONIST. DON'T GO IN THINKING THEY'RE GOING TO GIVE YOU YOUR OWN SHOW WITHIN YOUR FIRST SIX MONTHS.

EXPERIENCE IN THIS INDUSTRY IS GOLDEN, FROM A PERSONAL PERSPECTIVE. YOU'LL BE BETTER OFF IF YOU DON'T GO IN EXPECTING TO KNOW EVERYTHING OR EXPECTING TO IMPRESS EVERYONE AROUND YOU.

KELLYE PERDUE
STORYBOARD ARTIST ON *INFINITY TRAIN*
GREW UP IN DETROIT, MICHIGAN
STUDIED ILLUSTRATION AT THE
COLLEGE FOR CREATIVE STUDIES

I THINK IT'S WHAT EVERYONE ELSE SAYS : THAT IT'S A LOT OF TIMING AND LUCK. I'M A BELIEVER IN "IF IT'S MEANT TO HAPPEN IT'S GOING TO HAPPEN." IF YOU PUT THE WORK IN, SOMETHING IS GOING TO COME FROM IT.

I WOULD SUGGEST NOT MOVING OUT HERE WITHOUT A JOB UNLESS YOU HAVE A WAY TO SURVIVE UNTIL YOU LAND ONE (STAY WITH FRIENDS OR RELATIVES, WORK A DIFFERENT JOB, ETC.).

IT TOOK ME A YEAR AND A HALF TO LAND A FULL-TIME JOB IN A STUDIO. WAITING WAS PROBABLY BEST, EVEN THOUGH IT WAS STRESSFUL HAVING MY PARENTS ON MY BACK WHILE I WAS LIVING WITH THEM, DOING FREELANCE, SAVING MY MONEY, AND APPLYING TO JOBS.

MY FRIEND RECOMMENDED ME FOR MY FIRST STORYBOARD JOB. THEY TESTED ME, I DID A SKYPE INTERVIEW, AND THEY ASKED ME TO TRY AN EPISODE, FREELANCE, FROM DETROIT.

Yes!

AFTER I FINISHED THE EPISODE I WAS EXPECTING TO KNOW IF THEY'D HIRE ME OR NOT, BUT INSTEAD IT FELT LIKE,

WE REALLY LIKE YOUR STUFF, BUT WE'RE NOT SURE IF WE WANT TO HIRE YOU FULL-TIME, SO WE'LL KEEP GIVING YOU EPISODES AND SEE WHAT HAPPENS.

I HONESTLY DIDN'T LIKE IT.
I FELT LIKE I WAS BEING LEAD ON.

IT WAS ALSO VERY ANXIETY-INDUCING.
MY PARENTS WERE ASKING,

IS THIS HAPPENING? ARE THEY GOING TO HIRE YOU? YOU SHOULD GO OUT THERE AND ASK THEM WHAT'S GOING ON.

SO THAT'S WHAT I DID —
I FLEW OUT HERE AND CONFRONTED THEM AND ASKED THE DIRECTOR IF I WAS GOING TO GET THE JOB, AND THEY SAID "NO." I FLEW OUT HERE TO GET A NO.

WOULD YOU RECOMMEND PEOPLE GO TO ART SCHOOL IF THEY WANT TO WORK IN ANIMATION?

REALISTICALLY, I WOULD SAY "NO." I WAS REALLY LUCKY BECAUSE I WAS ABLE TO GET SCHOLAR-SHIPS, SO I STILL HAVE LOANS, BUT THEY'RE ALL FEDERAL. I FEEL REALLY LUCKY COMPARED TO MY CLASSMATES WHO HAVE HUNDREDS OF DOLLARS EVERY MONTH IN LOANS TO PAY BACK.

I'M NOT GOOD AT ONLINE CLASSES, SO HAVING A PLACE I COULD GO WAS AN ADDED BENEFIT. ALSO FOR IN-PERSON FRIENDSHIPS AND NETWORKING. IF YOU WANT TO LEARN THE BASICS YOU CAN STILL GO TO COMMUNITY COLLEGE. AND THERE ARE SO MANY RESOURCES ONLINE — SCHOOLISM, CGMA, IANIMATE, ANIMMENTOR. BUT REALLY, YOU NEED TO APPLY YOURSELF EITHER WAY.

I WOULD SUGGEST SCHOOLS LIKE CDA AND GNOMAN AND BRAINSTORM, BUT THEY'RE IN SUCH EXPENSIVE CITIES, IF YOU'RE A KID FROM ALABAMA, HOW ARE YOU GOING TO MOVE OUT HERE?! AND SOME ART SCHOOLS ARE SHAMS, OR PREDATORY. THEY SAY THEY'LL TEACH YOU ANIMATION BUT THEY'RE IN THE MIDDLE OF NOWHERE AND THEIR PROFESSORS HAVEN'T WORKED IN THE INDUSTRY IN 10 YEARS. DO YOUR RESEARCH. THINK REALISTICALLY : CAN I AFFORD THIS? WOULD THIS WORK OUT FOR ME IN THE LONG RUN? WILL THIS SCHOOL GIVE ME THE SKILLS I NEED SO WHEN I GRADUATE I HAVE A DECENT SHOT AT GETTING WORK?

ART SCHOOL?

GET A DAY JOB?

GET A DEGREE IN SOMETHING ELSE?

NO ART SCHOOL?

MOVE TO A BIG CITY?

I FEEL LIKE ONLINE IS THE BEST, ESPECIALLY IF YOU'RE NOT WILLING TO TAKE THE DEBT, OR YOU'RE NOT GIVEN THE OPPORTUNITY THROUGH SCHOLARSHIPS TO ALLEVIATE THE DEBT. IT'S A TRICKY SITUATION. IT'S TOTALLY NOT FAIR AT ALL. I THINK PEOPLE REALIZE THAT AND THAT'S WHY THEY FREAK OUT.

DEGREES DON'T MATTER AS MUCH HERE. I DON'T WANT TO SAY THEY'RE USELESS, BECAUSE THEY DO MATTER IN OTHER PLACES AND FOR OTHER PEOPLE. BUT, ME BEING BLACK, IF I DIDN'T HAVE A DEGREE, WHO KNOWS WHO WOULD TAKE ME ON. MAYBE IN ANIMATION, BUT MAYBE NOT SOMEWHERE ELSE. FOR BETTER OR FOR WORSE, IT'S LIKE A STAMP OF "I'M COMPETENT." IN A WAY IT HELPS PEOPLE TO SEE THAT YOU'RE SERIOUS BECAUSE YOU PUT ON ALL THIS DEBT AND WENT THROUGH THIS 4-YEAR INSTITUTION.

Kellye Perdue is SERIOUS about art!

THE BEST PART ABOUT WORKING IN ANIMATION IS THE PEOPLE. IT'S EASIER TO RELATE TO OTHER ARTISTS THAN NON-ARTISTS. EVERYONE IS LOOKING AT THINGS THROUGH AN ART-LENS / ARTIST PERSPECTIVE / A CERTAIN PERSONALITY THAT COMES FROM BEING IN THIS INDUSTRY THAT MESHES WELL WITH WORKING WITH DIFFERENT PEOPLE. WE'RE NOT ALL CLONES. WE'RE ALL WEIRD, AWKWARD ARTISTS, AND THAT MAKES A COMMUNITY.

I GUESS THE BAD THING IS WE'RE ALL AWKWARD ARTISTS. I'M LEARNING I HAVE TO REACH OUT MORE. NORMALLY I'M PRETTY SHY, SO I DON'T REACH OUT TO OTHER PEOPLE, I'VE ALWAYS HAD PEOPLE REACH OUT TO ME. IF YOU'RE REALLY RESERVED AND MAYBE YOU'RE NOT THE PERSON IN YOUR FRIEND GROUP TO MAKE PLANS, OR IT TAKES YOU A WHILE TO WARM UP TO PEOPLE, I WOULD SAY LEARN TO OPEN YOURSELF UP MORE, CUZ IT'S REALLY **LONELY!**

ALSO PEOPLE LIKE TO PLAN THINGS MORE HERE, IT'S NOT AS SPONTANEOUS. A LOT OF PEOPLE WOULD PREFER TO JUST GO HOME. KEEP THAT IN MIND, THE SOCIAL ASPECT IN ANIMATION IS TRICKY. IT'S NOT LIKE PEOPLE ARE EVIL, IT'S MORE LIKE PEOPLE KEEP TO THEMSELVES, AND I'M THE SAME, I LIKE BEING ALONE SOMETIMES, BUT I THOUGHT I WOULD CONNECT MORE EASILY WITH PEOPLE AT WORK, AT LEAST, OR EVEN FRIENDS I HAVE HERE, BUT REALLY I FEEL THE SAME AS I DID BACK HOME. HOW DID THEY ALL GET THEIR OWN LIVES?

I'VE BEEN ON THIS ANTI-L.A. KICK LATELY, WHERE THERE'S JUST NOTHING ABOUT THIS CITY THAT MAKES ME WANT TO LIVE HERE. PEOPLE ARE LIKE,

WELL WHY DON'T YOU JUST LEAVE?

BECAUSE I **WORK** HERE. WHERE ELSE AM I GOING TO WORK?

I MEAN, I WOULD IF I REALISTICALLY COULD. YOU NEED A CAR TO MOVE AROUND HERE. EVERYONE'S VERY DISTANT. IT'S NOT LIKE IN NEW YORK, WHERE AT LEAST YOU HAVE A TRAIN SYSTEM AND YOU CAN WALK PLACES. HERE IT'S EITHER GET A CAR OR LEARN TO FLY, BASICALLY. EVEN WITH LYFT IT GETS REALLY GETS EXPENSIVE. I MEAN, THE FOOD IS GOOD...OTHER THAN THAT, I WOULDN'T CALL THIS PLACE "HOME." I'M JUST LIVING HERE. EVERYONE'S LIKE, "GIVE IT 3 YEARS," BUT...THAT'S A REALLY LONG TIME.

YOU CAN'T FORCE THE FUTURE TO HAPPEN. YOU CAN'T FORCE CHANGE. YOU JUST HAVE TO BELIEVE IN YOUR ABILITY AND YOUR OWN SELF-WORTH THAT YOU WILL FIND SOMETHING. YEAH, IT'S GOING TO BE HARD AND IT'S GOING TO SUCK AND YOU'RE GOING TO BE LIKE "WHEN IS MY LIFE GOING TO BEGIN?!" BUT JUST STICK WITH IT.

MEGAN NAIRN,
STUDIO MANAGER AT
12FIELD ANIMATION
GREW UP IN KALBARRI,
AUSTRALIA
STUDIED MULTIMEDIA AT
SWINBURNE UNIVERSITY

MY VERY FIRST JOB IN ANIMATION WAS HELPING ONE OF MY UNIVERSITY LECTURERS "CLEAN UP" ANIMATION IN ADOBE ILLUSTRATOR FOR SOME ADS HE'D ANIMATED ON PAPER. I LEARNED A LOT FROM HIM, BUT HE WAS ALSO THE FIRST PERSON TO SCREW ME OVER BY NOT PAYING ME FOR COMMERCIAL WORK I'D DONE...SO I GUESS I LEARNED EVEN MORE THAN I BARGAINED FOR!

I WAS WORKING IN MELBOURNE, AUSTRALIA DOING A FEW DIFFERENT JOBS - TEACHING ANIMATION PART TIME, MAKING INTERACTIVE IPAD STORYBOOKS AND FREELANCE ANIMATION. THE INDUSTRY IS VERY DIFFERENT IN AUSTRALIA THAN IN L.A. MANY PEOPLE WORKING IN ANIMATION TEND TO DO A BIT OF EVERYTHING.

I DID A FEW FREELANCE ANIMATED E-CARDS FOR JIBJAB BROS STUDIOS. ONE DAY JIBJAB CALLED ME AND OFFERED ME A JOB IN HOUSE AT THEIR STUDIO IN L.A. IT HONESTLY WASN'T SOMETHING I WAS PLANNING ON, BUT IT WAS AN AMAZING OPPORTUNITY AND I WENT FOR IT!!! THEY SORTED OUT MY WORK VISA, I PACKED UP MY STUFF AND FLEW OVER TO MEET THEM IN PERSON FOR THE FIRST TIME AND TO START A WHOLE NEW LIFE IN THE U.S.A., **WOW!** SO THAT WAS PRETTY HUGE. A FEW YEARS LATER, I WAS OFFERED A JOB AT CARTOON NETWORK AS THE ANIMATION TALENT DEVELOPMENT MANAGER, WHICH CHANGED MY LIFE ONCE AGAIN.

CARTOON NETWORK BECAME INTERESTED IN ME THANKS TO ANIMATION SCREENINGS I'D BEEN ORGANIZING IN L.A. I'M PART OF AN ORGANIZATION CALLED LOOPDELOOP (BASED IN AUSTRALIA) THAT RUNS REGULAR ANIMATION CHALLENGES AND SCREENINGS. WHEN I MOVED TO L.A I IMPORTED IT WITH ME AND GOT SOME HELP TO START SCREENINGS THERE - THEY ARE STILL RUNNING REGULARLY NOW!

I'VE ALWAYS BEEN REALLY KEEN ON CONNECTING ANIMATORS TO EACH OTHER AND CREATING COMMUNITY AMONGST ARTISTS. PARTICIPATING IN LOOPDELOOP HAS BEEN GREAT FOR MY CAREER, AS WELL AS MANY OTHER ARTISTS AROUND THE WORLD.

I'M REALLY GLAD TO WORK IN THE ANIMATION INDUSTRY. HONESTLY, IT CAN BE TOUGH AND EXHAUSTING IN MANY DIFFERENT WAYS, BUT I STICK WITH IT BECAUSE I LOVE IT AND THE COMMUNITY OF ARTISTS INVOLVED IN IT. I'D DEFINITELY 100% ENCOURAGE YOUNG PEOPLE TO PURSUE A CAREER IN ANIMATION IF THEY HAVE A PASSION FOR DRAWINGS AND STORIES. IN FACT, PART OF MY JOB THESE DAYS **IS** ENCOURAGING OTHERS TO PURSUE JOBS IN ANIMATION!

THE WORST PART ABOUT LIVING IN L.A. WAS BEING SO FAR AWAY FROM MY FRIENDS, FAMILY AND ESTABLISHED SUPPORT NETWORK. COMING FROM AUSTRALIA, THE TIME ZONE DIFFERENCE WAS HUGE. IT WAS DIFFICULT TO EVEN FIND THE TIME TO CHAT ON THE PHONE WITH PEOPLE BACK HOME.

L.A.   MELBOURNE

ALSO DRIVING EVERYWHERE REALLY SUCKS.

THE BEST THING ABOUT LIFE IN L.A. IS HONESTLY - THE **WORK!!!** SO MANY ICONIC CARTOONS ARE MADE IN L.A. THERE'S A GREAT ENERGY ABOUT THAT - PEOPLE MOVE TO L.A. FOR THE WORK AND THEY ARE ENTHUSIASTIC, DRIVEN AND FULL OF ENERGY TO MAKE STUFF. ON TOP OF THAT, YOU HAVE THE CHANCE TO WORK WITH ARTISTS WHOM YOU'VE ALWAYS ADMIRED. I GREW UP IN A TINY TOWN IN AUSTRALIA, AND I ENDED UP WORKING IN A REALLY EXCITING ROLE IN A HUGE CITY!

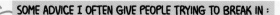

THE BEST PART ABOUT WORKING IN ANIMATION IS MAKING COOL STORIES AND BEING ABLE TO BRING SOMETHING TO LIFE FROM NOTHING! ANIMATION IS MAGICAL AND WE ARE SURROUNDED BY WIZARDS WHO CAN DRAW WORLDS THAT HAVE NEVER EXISTED, AND MAKE YOU FEEL THINGS FOR CHARACTERS WHO CAN JUST BE A SIMPLE SHAPES WITH EYES. ISN'T THAT **AMAZING!?** THE WORST PART ABOUT WORKING IN ANIMATION IN L.A., FOR ME, WAS HOW PEOPLE COULD BE OVERLY AMBITIOUS, AT A BIG COST TO THE PEOPLE AROUND THEM. IT CAN BE TOUGH TO SURVIVE IN A CREATIVE INDUSTRY, LET ALONE IN L.A., AND UNFORTUNATELY SOMETIMES THAT RESULTS IN PEOPLE PUTTING WORK FIRST ABOVE ALL ELSE - FROM PLACING THEIR WORK BEFORE FAMILY OR FRIENDSHIP, TO TREATING PEOPLE LIKE OBJECTS OR A RUNG ON THE CAREER LADDER RATHER THAN HUMAN BEINGS. PEOPLE CAN BURN OUT AND BECOME JADED AND SELFISH, OR ABUSE THEIR POWER AND SUCCESS TO TREAT OTHERS POORLY. WE DON'T NEED TO ALL BE THE HERO OR THE SHOWRUNNER OF A STORY, SOMETIMES HELPING SOMEONE ELSE TELL THEIR STORY IS EVEN MORE IMPORTANT.

SOME ADVICE I OFTEN GIVE PEOPLE TRYING TO BREAK IN :

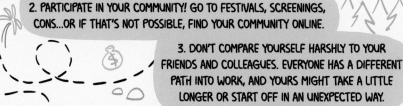

1. PORTFOLIOS ARE ABOUT QUALITY, NOT QUANTITY! PICK OUT YOUR STRONGEST PIECES AND CREATE A SITE FOCUSED ON THE BEST WORK YOU DO. ALWAYS MAKE SURE TO ADD AN EMAIL ADDRESS ON YOUR SOCIAL / BLOG / SITE SO PEOPLE CAN GET IN TOUCH.

2. PARTICIPATE IN YOUR COMMUNITY! GO TO FESTIVALS, SCREENINGS, CONS...OR IF THAT'S NOT POSSIBLE, FIND YOUR COMMUNITY ONLINE.

3. DON'T COMPARE YOURSELF HARSHLY TO YOUR FRIENDS AND COLLEAGUES. EVERYONE HAS A DIFFERENT PATH INTO WORK, AND YOURS MIGHT TAKE A LITTLE LONGER OR START OFF IN AN UNEXPECTED WAY.

4. KEEP ON MAKING YOUR OWN STUFF, NO MATTER WHAT!

SAM SPINA
STORY ARTIST ON *INFINITY TRAIN*
STUDIED GRAPHIC DESIGN AT THE
UNIVERSITY OF SOUTH CAROLINA
GREW UP IN ARIZONA AND
SOUTH CAROLINA

AFTER SCHOOL I WAS JUST WAITING TABLES AND DRAWING COMICS IN DENVER. I DIDN'T KNOW ANYTHING AT ALL ABOUT ANIMATION.

I HAPPENED TO MEET SOMEONE WHO WORKED AT NICKELODEON AT A COMIC CONVENTION I WAS TABLING AT, AND SHE TOLD ME ABOUT THEIR SHORTS PROGRAM. I PITCHED AND HAD A SHORT MADE ("HOLE", 2012)! THAT WAS SUCH A CRAZY, BACK-DOOR LOOK AT HOW IT ALL WORKED. I GOT TO SEE FIRSTHAND EVERY STEP OF MAKING A CARTOON. UNRELATED, BUT ALSO THROUGH MY MINI COMICS, I GOT A JOB ON *REGULAR SHOW* A COUPLE YEARS AFTER THAT.

WHEN I WAS A WAITER, MY CO-WORKERS WERE ALWAYS ASKING ME TO COME HANG OUT AND DRINK AFTER WORK AND STUFF – NOBODY UNDERSTOOD THE **HUSTLE** OF AN ARTIST.

EVENTUALLY PEOPLE LEARNED NOT TO ASK ME TO COME OVER AND WATCH MOVIES, HAHA. DENVER ACTUALLY HAD A REALLY COOL COMIC SCENE AND IT WAS NICE BEING AROUND LIKE-MINDED, BUSY PEOPLE. THAT'S SOMETHING I REALLY LIKE ABOUT L.A. – EVERYONE HAS THEIR OWN PERSONAL PROJECTS! EVERYONE IS A CREATIVE IN L.A. I LOVE LIVING HERE.

ONE OF THE OBVIOUS DRAWBACKS IS THAT IT'S **CRAZY**-EXPENSIVE, BUT THAT'S KIND OF EVERY BIG CITY RIGHT NOW. LIKE, I'M AT A POINT IN MY LIFE WHERE I COULD THINK ABOUT BUYING A HOUSE, BUT THERE'S NO WAY I COULD AFFORD TO HERE.

I'M NOT GOING TO COMPLAIN ABOUT TRAFFIC OR ANYTHING – I WALK TO WORK AND BIKE A LOT. PEOPLE THAT COMPLAIN ABOUT L.A. TRAFFIC SHOULD SPEND A DAY IN ATLANTA! NOW THAT'S TERRIBLE.

L.A. REALLY HAS TONS OF OPPORTUNITY, AND PEOPLE ARE A LOT NICER THAN I WOULD HAVE THOUGHT. I THOUGHT IT WOULD HAVE BEEN CUTTHROAT AND COMPETITIVE, BUT IT DOESN'T FEEL LIKE THAT AT ALL. EVERY-BODY'S SO FRIENDLY AND UPLIFTING.

EVEN PITCHING SHOWS SEEMS LIKE SUCH A CRAZY HOLLYWOOD THING, BUT IT'S REALLY NOT! EVERY EXECUTIVE I'VE WORKED WITH HAS BEEN A SURPRISINGLY CASUAL, NORMAL PERSON. THEY'RE ALSO VERY USED TO WORKING WITH AWKWARD ARTIST TYPES, HAHA. I CRINGE WHEN I THINK ABOUT HOW BADLY I'VE PITCHED SOME STUFF...BUT THEY UNDERSTAND THAT I'M JUST A WEIRDO AND CAN STILL APPRECIATE MY IDEAS.

NOD

ONE DOWNSIDE IS THAT DEADLINES ARE BRUTAL IN ANIMATION. LIKE, I HAD TO WORK ALL LAST WEEKEND. THE LAST SEASON OF *REGULAR SHOW* HAD A NICE PACE. WE'D GET TWO WEEKS OFF EVERY TWO EPISODES, SO YOU COULD RECHARGE. IT'D BE COOL IF THAT WAS BUILT INTO EVERY SHOW'S SCHEDULE. THIS JOB IS SUCH A ROLLER-COASTER, ONE WEEK IS SUPER CHILL, THE NEXT IS A NIGHTMARE. IT'S ALSO NOT THAT STABLE...I'VE BEEN LUCKY TO STAY AT CARTOON NETWORK FOR SO LONG, BUT IF MY SHOW ISN'T RENEWED THIS FALL, I'M OUT OF A JOB.

WE HAVE UNPAID HIATUSES BETWEEN SEASONS. I JUST HAD SIX WEEKS OFF, WHICH CAN BE TOUGH FINANCIALLY, BUT IT'S ALSO THE FREAKING **BEST!** IT RULES TO HAVE A LONG BREAK WHEN YOU KNOW YOU'RE COMING BACK. IT GIVES YOU TIME TO TRAVEL AND DO PERSONAL PROJECTS AND STUFF.

I COME FROM MINI COMICS AND ZINES, WHERE YOU TELL YOU OWN STORIES, SO WHENEVER I GET ASKED, "WHAT SCHOOL DO I GO TO TO GET INTO ANIMATION?" I JUST TELL THEM TO WRITE A LOT AND MAKE AS MUCH STUFF AS POSSIBLE. IT'S HARD TO GIVE DEFINITIVE ADVICE LIKE THAT, BUT THAT WAS MY WAY IN. I NEVER HAD AN END-GOAL FOR MAKING MY COMICS. I WAS TRULY MAKING THEM BECAUSE I WAS COMPELLED TO MAKE THEM. I FEEL LIKE IF YOU DO THINGS THAT WAY, YOU CAN'T FAIL!

LIKE IF ANIMATION IS YOUR PASSION AND YOU WOULD BE HAPPY DOING IT EVEN IF IT WASN'T YOUR FULL-TIME JOB, THEN ABSOLUTELY GO FOR IT! MAYBE IT'S JUST A HOBBY AND YOU HAVE TO WORK AT A RESTAURANT TO PAY THE BILLS, THAT'S COOL TOO. BUT SERIOUSLY, IF YOU JUST CONTINUE TO MAKE LOTS OF STUFF, EVENTUALLY PEOPLE WILL NOTICE.

AND IN CONCLUSION...WHAT IS YOUR FAVORITE THING TO DO IN L.A. IF YOU HAVE A FREE DAY?

I WOULD JUST SPEND THE DAY GOING TO A POLE DANCE STUDIO AND DOING THAT THE ENTIRE DAY!

I WOULD TAKE A SKETCHPAD AND GO DRAWING. THE GROVE IS AWESOME, AND THE BEACH, BOARDWALK, PIER, OR A COFFEE SHOP.

GO THE BEACH WITH MY KIDS AND HAVE AN ICE CREAM AT JENI'S ON HILLHURST. OR GO BOULDERING AT L.A. BOULDERS IN D.T.L.A., THEN BRUNCH AT THE MESSHALL WITH FRIENDS!

GO TO A NEW PLACE AND JUST WALK AND SEE WHAT'S AROUND! I LIKE WANDERING INTO STORES AND PARKS AND TO GET A LITTLE EXERCISE.

LITTLE TOKYO! IF YOU LIKE GREAT JAPANESE FOOD AND NERDY ANIME FIGURES AND GOODS, IT'S A GREAT PLACE TO GO WITH FRIENDS AND HANG OUT FOR AN AFTERNOON.

I WOULD GO HANG AROUND ECHO PARK LAKE WITH AN ICE COFFEE AND SOME DONUTS. I'D DEFINITELY EAT SOME DELICIOUS TACOS, AND TRY AND CATCH A GIG.

  ha ha

I'D PROBABLY JUST HANG OUT WITH FRIENDS. I FEEL LIKE I'M TOO NEW HERE TO ANSWER THAT QUESTION.

ME AND MY WIFE LOVE TO GO TO COMEDY SHOWS. THEY ARE AMAZING, AND THEY'RE, LIKE, FREE OR $5 HERE!

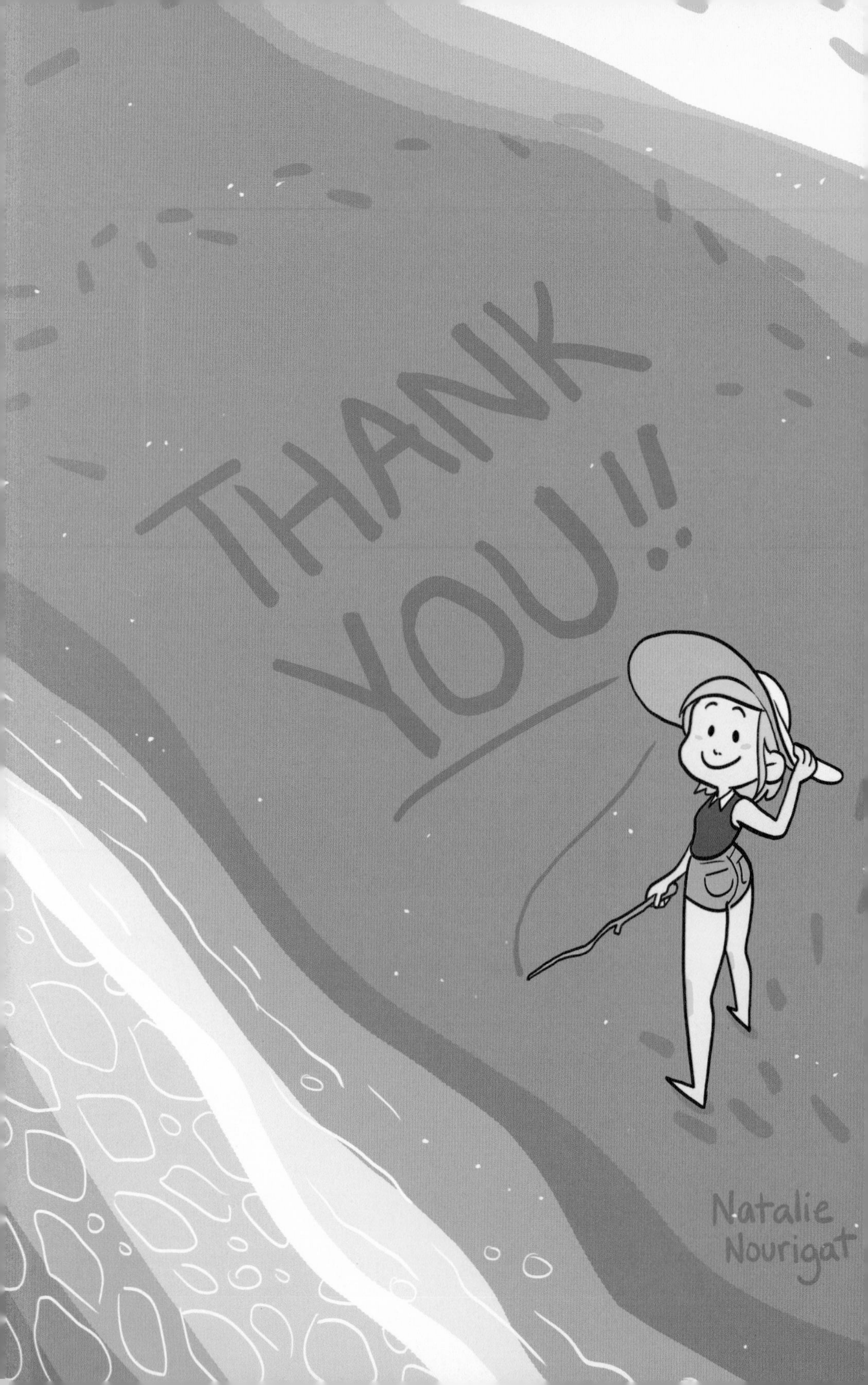
THANK YOU!!
Natalie Nourigat

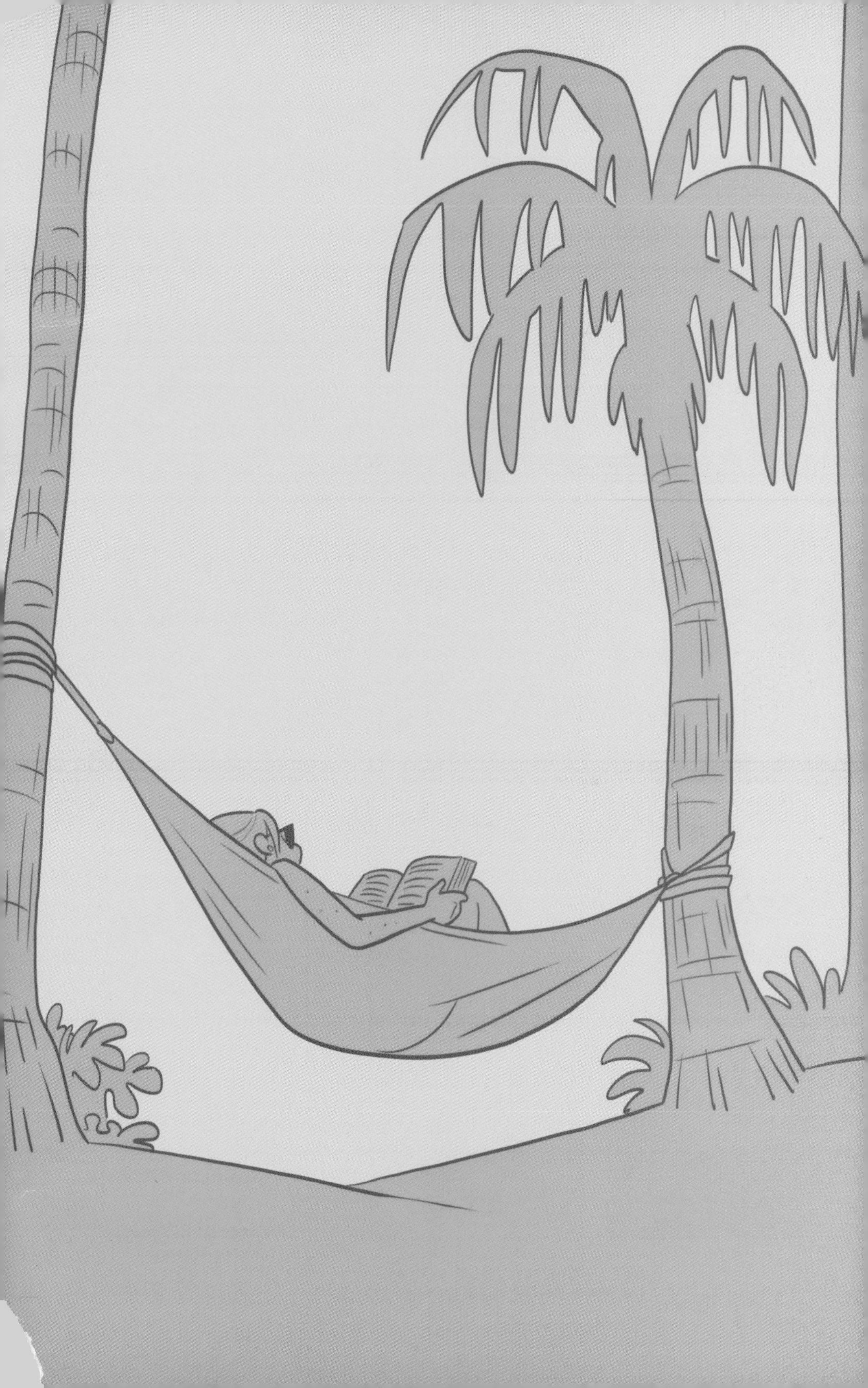

DISCOVER
ALL THE HITS

Lumberjanes
Noelle Stevenson, Shannon Watters, Grace Ellis, Brooklyn Allen, and Others
Volume 1: Beware the Kitten Holy
ISBN: 978-1-60886-687-8 | $14.99 US
Volume 2: Friendship to the Max
ISBN: 978-1-60886-737-0 | $14.99 US
Volume 3: A Terrible Plan
ISBN: 978-1-60886-803-2 | $14.99 US
Volume 4: Out of Time
ISBN: 978-1-60886-860-5 | $14.99 US
Volume 5: Band Together
ISBN: 978-1-60886-919-0 | $14.99 US

Giant Days
John Allison, Lissa Treiman, Max Sarin
Volume 1
ISBN: 978-1-60886-789-9 | $9.99 US
Volume 2
ISBN: 978-1-60886-804-9 | $14.99 US
Volume 3
ISBN: 978-1-60886-851-3 | $14.99 US

Jonesy
Sam Humphries, Caitlin Rose Boyle
Volume 1
ISBN: 978-1-60886-883-4 | $9.99 US
Volume 2
ISBN: 978-1-60886-999-2 | $14.99 US

Slam!
Pamela Ribon, Veronica Fish, Brittany Peer
Volume 1
ISBN: 978-1-68415-004-5 | $14.99 US

Goldie Vance
Hope Larson, Brittney Williams
Volume 1
ISBN: 978-1-60886-898-8 | $9.99 US
Volume 2
ISBN: 978-1-60886-974-9 | $14.99 US

The Backstagers
James Tynion IV, Rian Sygh
Volume 1
ISBN: 978-1-60886-993-0 | $14.99 US

Tyson Hesse's Diesel: Ignition
Tyson Hesse
ISBN: 978-1-60886-907-7 | $14.99 US

Coady & The Creepies
Liz Prince, Amanda Kirk, Hannah Fisher
ISBN: 978-1-68415-029-8 | $14.99 US